SSL VPN

Understanding, evaluating, and planning secure, web-based remote access

Joseph Steinberg
Timothy Speed

[PACKT]
PUBLISHING

SSL VPN
Understanding, evaluating, and planning secure, web-based remote access

First edition: February 2005

Published by Packt Publishing Ltd.
32 Lincoln Road
Olton
Birmingham, B27 6PA, UK.

ISBN 1-904811-07-8

www.packtpub.com

Cover Design by www.visionwt.com

Credits

Authors
Joseph Steinberg
Timothy Speed

Commissioning Editor
David Barnes

Technical Editors*
Chris Fernando
Ashutosh Pande

Layout*
Nanda Padmanabhan

Indexer*
Ashutosh Pande

Proofreader
Chris Smith

Cover Designer
Helen Wood

*   Services provided by Editorialindia.com

About the Authors

Joseph Steinberg has been involved with computer networking and security since 1989. He has worked in technical positions at Citibank and AT&T and served in senior-management capacities at several product vendors and consulting firms. He has spent more than four years with Whale Communications, one of the pioneers of SSL VPN technology.

Mr. Steinberg's May 2003 article, *SSL VPN Security*, introduced an awareness of critical security issues created by SSL VPN technology; since its publication, nearly every SSL VPN vendor has acted upon the concerns and recommendations made in the article.

Mr. Steinberg earned an M.S. in Computer Science from NYU, and holds a CISSP (Certified Information Systems Security Professional) credential as well as advanced certifications in IT security management (ISSMP) and architecture (ISSAP). He has lectured on several topics related to IT security and management and has authored numerous articles that have appeared in various journals, magazines, and other publications. A recognized expert on IT security, he is also interviewed on a regular basis by media personalities and is a member of several panels discussing IT-security related matters.

Mr. Steinberg lives in the suburbs of New York City with his wife and two daughters.

To Shira, Penina Leora, and Miriam, with all my love.

Timothy Speed is an IBM-Certified IT Architect working for the IBM Lotus Brand (ISSL). Tim has been involved in Internet and messaging security since 1992. He also participated with the Domino infrastructure team at the Nagano Olympics and with the Lotus Notes systems for the Sydney Olympics. His certifications include CISSP, MCSE, A+ Plus Security from CompTIA, Lotus Domino CLP Principal Administrator, and Lotus Domino CLP Principal Developer. (Notes/Domino certifications in R3, R4, R5, and ND6)

Tim has also co-authored four books:

- *The Internet Security Guidebook*, ISBN: 0-12-237471-1, February, 2001
- *The Personal Internet Security Guidebook*, ISBN: 0-12-656561-9, October, 2001
- *Enterprise Directory and Security Implementation Guide: Designing and Implementing Directories in Your Organization*, ISBN: 0-12-160452-7
- *Internet Security: A Jumpstart for Systems Administrators and IT Managers*, ISBN: 1-55558-298-2

I am grateful to Joseph Steinberg for asking me to participate in writing this book. Special thanks to David Barnes, Commissioning Editor, Packt Publishing. Thanks to IBM/ISSL, Steve Keohane, Kathrine Rutledge, Chris Cotton, and Jack Shoemaker for allowing me to co-author this book. Thanks to Ann Marie Darrough for the official IBM review of this book before publishing.

Also thanks to the following:

The great Shane George, Tery W. Corkran, Chuck Stauber, David Byrd, David Bell, Dick McCarrick, Frederic Dahm, Garry White, Hartmut Samtleben, Hissan C. Waheed, Raj Balasubramanian, Ralph Vawter, William Nunez, Steve Robinson, Larry Berthelsen, Brian Baker, Lillian Speed, Johnny Speed, and Katherine Speed.

To Linda Speed, still my favorite wife!

Table of Contents

Introduction

The advent of SSL VPN ushers in a new era in remote computing. Where older remote-access technologies were expensive, complicated to use, and often deployed to only limited user populations, SSL VPN delivers remote access to the masses at a much lower cost than its forerunners, and in a much simpler format. It transforms remote access from a convenience enjoyed by a select few to a mainstream business option available to everyone.

An exciting new technology, SSL VPN leverages web browsers to provide access to enterprise applications, systems, files, and other resources from essentially any Internet-connected web browser, abandoning the long-standing model of requiring specialized client software to enable remote access.

SSL VPN offers several significant benefits over previous generations of remote access tools. Typically:

- It is much easier to use.
- It is much easier to implement and maintain.
- It offers access from many more locations and devices.
- It is much less expensive to maintain.
- It can serve as an integral component of a business-continuity strategy.

As of the publishing of this book, several key analyst firms have issued reports on the SSL VPN market; while they may differ in the rankings of the vendors in the space, they are all in agreement that SSL VPN is gaining rapid acceptance into corporate infrastructures. Annual SSL VPN related revenue, which exploded in 2002-2003, continues to grow at a healthy pace.

What This Book Covers

In this book, SSL VPN is discussed in detail from both a business and technical standpoint. Readers will gain understanding of what SSL VPN is, how it works, and why it may be of great benefit to their own organizations. Best practices surrounding deploying an SSL VPN, ensuring that an SSL VPN implementation is secure, as well as addressing human factors are also covered.

Chapter 1 introduces the key concepts behind SSL VPN. We look at how it fits into familiar network schemas, and consider how it works and what advantages it offers over tradition IPSec VPNs.

Then, in *Chapter 2*, we consider the business case for SSL VPN solutions. We see how to measure SSL VPN return on investment, and what practical benefits SSL VPN technology can offer an organization.

Chapter 3 peeks under the bonnet of SSL VPN to see how the technology works, and how you can rely on private communications over an open network like the Internet.

Chapter 4 takes a more detailed look at SSL VPN security, showing you how to make sure you choose SSL VPN tools and configurations that do not fall foul of glitches or security loopholes.

Chapter 5 looks at how to plan your SSL VPN installation by showing where it fits into your current network infrastructure, while *Chapter 6* looks at the human angle—how to educate your users so that they do not become security holes themselves!

Worried that an SSL VPN will not work with your existing applications? In *Chapter 7* we look at the methods that exist for integrating SSL VPN with your legacy applications.

Finally in *Chapter 8* we look to the future of SSL VPN, and consider where the trends are likely to lead in the coming years.

Conventions

In this book you will find a number of styles of text that distinguish between different kinds of information. Here are some examples of these styles, and an explanation of their meanings.

Code words in text are shown as follows: "NOCACHE does not prevent caching in AutoComplete stores, in history records, and other areas."

New terms and **important words** are introduced in a bold-type font. Words that you see on the screen—in menus or dialog boxes, for example—appear in the text as follows: Are you still there?

> Tips, suggestions, or important notes appear in a box like this.

Reader Feedback

Feedback from our readers is always welcome. Let us know what you think about this book, what you liked or may have disliked. Reader feedback is important for us to develop titles that you really get the most out of.

To send us general feedback, simply drop an e-mail to feedback@packtpub.com, making sure to mention the book title in the subject of your message.

If there is a book that you need and would like to see us publish, please send us a note in the Suggest a title form on www.packtpub.com or e-mail suggest@packtpub.com.

If there is a topic that you have expertise in and you are interested in either writing or contributing to a book, see our author guide on www.packtpub.com/authors.

Customer Support

Now that you are the proud owner of a Packt book, we have a number of things to help you to get the most from your purchase.

Errata

Although we have taken every care to ensure the accuracy of our contents, mistakes do happen. If you find a mistake in one of our books—maybe a mistake in text or code—we would be grateful if you would report this to us. By doing this you can save other readers from frustration, and also help to improve subsequent versions of this book.

If you find any errata, report them by visiting http://www.packtpub.com/support, selecting your book, clicking on the Submit Errata link, and entering the details of your errata. Once your errata have been verified, your submission will be accepted and the errata added to the list of existing errata. The existing errata can be viewed by selecting your title from http://www.packtpub.com/support.

Questions

You can contact us at questions@packtpub.com if you are having a problem with some aspect of the book, and we will do our best to address it.

1

Introduction to SSL VPN

History provides us with a map of how technology effectuates changes in the way we live and work. This technological transformation started with simple tools that then expanded to the internal combustion engine and now to the technology of computers and networks. One important example of this is transportation. Through a system of physical networks—roads, trains, airplanes, and so on—people can now work and live outside the congestion of large cities. Large parts of the population moved to 'suburb communities', and started the famous daily commute. In spite of high petrol prices, people stayed in their suburbs. Today, with the advent of the Internet, people can work almost anywhere. One of the technologies that allow the ubiquitous access required is a technology known as SSL VPN. This chapter starts you on the knowledge roads that will educate you about this technology. Nevertheless, before we get into too much detail, let's first understand how this technology will help you.

Many people work for what is now known as a 'virtual' organization. Workers in a virtual organization will not necessarily need an office, cube, or a parking space. More and more companies are letting staffers work remotely. The term used to describe these types of worker is teleworkers. As per the **ITAC (International Telework Association and Council)**, the number of U.S. employees who work remotely has grown every year since 1999. The ITAC commissioned a study conducted by Dieringer Research Group (statistically based on teleworkers working at least one day per month), which shows teleworking has grown by nearly forty percent since 2001. What makes teleworking possible is the ability to connect your computer to the Internet from anywhere, anytime. This process of connecting remotely to the Internet is easy, and now with wireless, access is ubiquitous. Teleworking and remote computing is more than just working from poolside at your ranch house. It includes:

- Drinking coffee while working on a laptop at the local coffee shop (wireless 802.11)
- Reading your online mail while on a train to a customer
- On a customer site, using their network to connect to your corporate network

- Sitting on a flight to Frankfurt—updating your résumé, and posting it to an Internet-based job site
- Accessing accounting data via the Internet café on 42nd street in New York
- Playing online games sitting on your deck in the backyard (with your dog)
- Working from your house with the white picket fence in the suburbs

---

Wireless Network

A wireless LAN is just that—wireless. Computers and routers will connect to each other via a set protocol and via a Radio Frequency circuit. Much like TV or your cell phone, your home network can connect computers together without wires. The name of the wireless networking protocol is **IEEE 802.11**. This standard was developed to maximize interoperability between differing brands of wireless LANs (WLANs). The 802.11 technologies can work with standard Ethernet via a bridge or **Access Point (AP)**. Wireless Ethernet uses a **Carrier Sense Multiple Access with Collision Avoidance (CSMA/CA)** scheme, whereas standard Ethernet uses a **Carrier Sense Multiple Access with Collision Detection (CSMA/CD)** scheme. One of the biggest advantages the 802.11 standard is the ability for products from different vendors to interoperate with each other. This means that as a user, you can purchase a wireless LAN card from one vendor and a wireless LAN card from another vendor and they can communicate with each other, independent of the brand name of the card.

Now you can be online almost anywhere and anytime. There are very few limits to *anywhere* with wireless access in North America, Asia, and Europe, and soon you will be able to *Google* from anywhere in the world. So as you can see, all is happy and secure in the world of ubiquitous Internet access. OK, let us stop and review that last statement. We used the words: 'anytime' and 'anywhere'; so far, so good. The word *secure* is not always true. In fact, with today's Internet, the traffic is rarely secure. The days of the 9600-baud modem are gone, along with the naive attitude that "all is secure". Access to the Internet is no longer safe.

The Internet is the communication backbone for more than just e-commerce; today you can access the Internet for almost everything:

- Playing online games, posting your résumé, and looking for new loves
- Supporting your business:
  - B2B (Business to Business)
  - B2C (Business to Consumer)
  - B2E (Business to Employee)

- Messaging and emailing (with all of that spam…)

The Internet

In order to understand the security issues of the Internet, you first need to understand what the Internet really is. The Internet is not just *one* network. The Internet includes thousands of individual networks. The communication core of these networks is two protocols known as **Transmission Control Protocol** and **Internet Protocol (TCP/IP)**. These historic protocols provide connectivity between equipment from many vendors over a variety of networking technologies. The **Transmission Control Protocol (TCP)** is intended for use as a highly reliable host-to-host protocol in a packet-switched computer communication network. The **Internet Protocol (IP)** is specifically limited in scope to provide the functions necessary to deliver an envelope of data from one computer system to another. Each computer or device on a network will have some type of address that identifies where it is on the network.

Much like computers, the Internet is a new concept for the world of communication. In 1973 Vinton Cerf, a UCLA (University of California, Los Angeles) graduate student who is also known as the *Father of the Internet*, and Robert Kahn, an MIT (Massachusetts Institute of Technology) math professor, developed a set of software *protocols* to enable different types of computers to exchange data. The software they developed is now known as TCP/IP. The base part of the protocol is called IP or Internet Protocol. While the IP part of the protocol transports the packets of data between the various computer systems on the Internet, the TCP part ports data to the applications. TCP is the mechanism that allows the **WWW (World Wide Web)** to communicate. (All of this will be discussed in detail later in this book.) Programs are built on top of this medium, which allows communication between server and client. A network can be connected with cables and/or wireless adapters. Basically the computer is connected via a **Network Interface Card (NIC)**. The NIC card's job is to place data into the network. All network data is crafted into packets and each packet has the information needed to find its target computer and knows where it came from.

Reference Models

The process of creating data packets is based on two connection models—the OSI and DARPA reference models. The **Open Systems Interconnection (OSI)** model is a standard reference model for how network data is transmitted between any two points in a computer network. TCP/IP in its most basic form supports the **Defense Advanced Research Projects Agency (DARPA)** model of internetworking and its network-defined layers. Much like the DARPA model, the OSI was designed to connect dissimilar computer network systems. The OSI reference model defines seven layers of functions that take place at each end of a network communication:

OSI Reference Model

Layer	Description
Application (7)	This is the layer at which programs are identified; user authentication and privacy are implemented here.
Presentation (6)	This is a layer—usually part of an operating system—that converts incoming and outgoing data from one presentation format to another.
Session (5)	This layer sets up, coordinates, ends conversations, exchanges, and dialogs between the applications at each end of the dialog.
Transport (4)	This layer manages the end-to-end control and error checking.
Network (3)	This layer handles the routing and forwarding of the data.
Data link (2)	This layer provides error control and synchronization for the physical level.
Physical (1)	This layer transmits the bit stream through the network at the electrical and mechanical level.

TCP/IP also has a much simpler protocol model called the DARPA model:

DARPA Model

Layer	Description
Process (4)	This is the layer where higher-level processes such as FTP, SMTP, and HTTP are defined and executed.
Host to Host (3)	This is where TCP lives. This is the mechanism that actually ports the data to the correct application. TCP ports are defined here.
Internet (2)	IP addresses are used to direct packets to the correct destination. Routing protocols live here along with **Address Resolution Protocol (ARP)** and **Internet Control Message Protocol (ICMP)**.
Network Interface (1)	This is the physical connection to the network: Ethernet, token ring, and so on. The packets are placed onto the network at this point.

Introducing Hacker Bob

Network architecture is discussed in detail in Appendix A. It is important for you to understand network architecture, since hackers understand it! Hacking into computers can include TCP port scanning, fake emails, trojans, and IP address spoofing. The essence of TCP port surfing is to pick out a target computer and explore it to see what ports are open and what a hacker can do with them. If you understand ports then you can understand what hackers can do to you and your systems. With this knowledge you can understand how to effectively keep your computers and networks secure.

Next is our introduction to Hacker Bob.

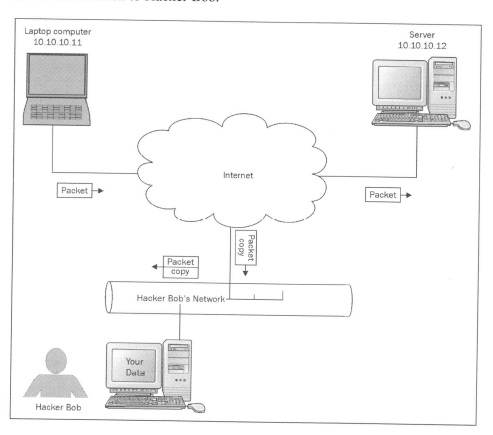

The above figure shows how Hacker Bob uses his evil hacker tools (and experience) to monitor your network.

Remember those packets and TCP ports? Hacker Bob can monitor the Internet and copy packets into his evil network. Once he has the copied packets, then he can analyze them and extract your sensitive data as explained below:

Trapping Your Data

Once Hacker Bob has your data then he can use a simple tool to review and analyze it. The following example shows how Hacker Bob could analyze your IP packet:

1. The user launched a browser and entered the following site: `http://www.HR_Data_the_company.xyz`.

2. Hacker Bob was monitoring the Internet with a **network packet capture** utility.

3. Bob was able to use a filter to view just port 80 packets (HTTP only).

4. Bob then viewed the IP packet payload.

In this example below, the data section is 1460 bytes. This payload is transferred in ASCII text using HTML. As a result, it is easy for Hacker Bob to read the data:

`</font><b><font color="#424282">@This data is a Secret</font>`

Now in the hacker's words "That data is mine."

```
⊞ Frame 15 (1514 bytes on wire, 1514 bytes captured)
⊞ Ethernet II, Src: 00:90:27:86:24:94, Dst: 00:0c:f1:0c:d3:2c
⊞ Internet Protocol, Src Addr: 192.9.200.100 (192.9.200.100), Dst Addr: 192.9.200.30 (192.9.200.30)
⊞ Transmission Control Protocol, Src Port: http (80), Dst Port: 3404 (3404), Seq: 2382796266, Ack:
⊟ Hypertext Transfer Protocol
    Data (1460 bytes)


        </font><b><font color="#424282">@This data is a Secret</font>
```

Basic HTTP Authentication

To make things worse, at some point, during your normal Internet browsing activities, you have likely received one of these types of pop-up windows from your browser:

Typically the username is some name that an administrator (or software utility) has assigned to you or you have assigned yourself. The Web is full of places that require a username. The username is a mechanism that identifies who you are in relation to the program or data you are trying to access. The password is the key that proves that you have the authority to use that username. This is a simple and effective mechanism to access controlled data. In Basic HTTP Authentication, the password passed over the network is neither encrypted nor plain text, but is 'uuencoded'. Anyone watching packet traffic on the network will see the password encoded in a simple format that is easily decoded by anyone who happens to catch the right network packet. Therefore, our friend Hacker Bob could just extract the right packet and he has your username and password. All Hacker Bob had to do was to read RFC2617 (`http://www.ietf.org/rfc/rfc2617.txt`) for all the information he needed.

Keeping Hacker Bob Out of Your Data

Here is the scenario: you are the network manager of a large worldwide enterprise company. You know that you must provide secure access from about 50 sites from around the world to your corporate networking at your headquarters in Dallas. In addition, each site will have a local network with about 10-12 computers each. Making your task a bit harder, the CIO of your company has mandated that you must save money and, at the same time, quickly get the network service up and running. How can you do this? One answer to this problem would be to set up direct connect circuits to each site, also known as a private network. However, this can be a really expensive solution. So, the solution to this quagmire is obvious—you can create a **Virtual Private Network (VPN)**.

VPNs

You now ask: "So what is a VPN?" The most basic definition of a VPN is "a *secure* connection between two or more locations over some type of a public network". A more detailed definition of a VPN is a private data network that makes use of the public communication infrastructure. A VPN can provide secure data transmission by tunneling data between two points—that is it uses encryption to ensure that no systems other than those at the endpoints can understand the communications. The following diagram shows a basic example:

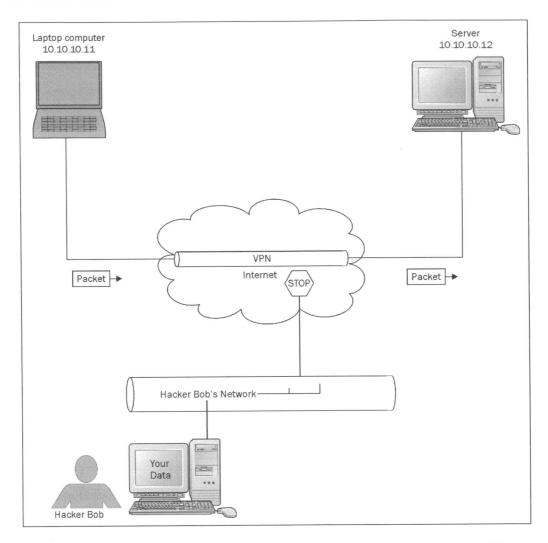

Traveling sales people will connect to the Internet via a local provider. This provider can be AOL, EarthLink, a local community Internet Service Provider (also known as a **POP—Point Of Presence**). The diagram above shows the concept of the VPN. The VPN now hides, or encrypts, the data, thus keeping Hacker Bob out of your data.

Remember your challenge from the CIO—"secure access from 50 sites around the world into the corporate network and each site having about 10-12 computers?" We have the answer for you. Let's look at two examples:

- Connecting one computer to the company corporate network

- Connecting networks together (your answer)

One Computer to the Corporate Network

In the example, below, a traveling user is able to connect securely to the corporate network via the VPN. The user will connect to the VPN via a local Internet service provider, then that traffic will be routed to the corporate network. At this point the VPN traffic from the end user will terminate into a VPN receiving device or server.

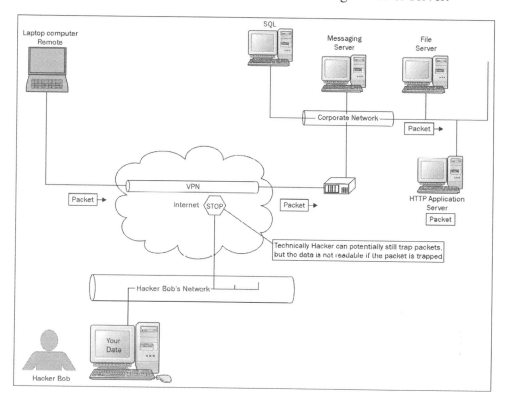

As you can see, Hacker Bob cannot read and/or trap your data—he is *stopped*.

> In this example above Hacker Bob may still be able to trap a copy of each packet, but the encrypted data will not be readable.

Remote Office Network Connected to the Main Office

In the example below, a remote office will be able to connect to the computers and servers in another office via the Internet. An end user on the remote network will access one of the corporate network services. The traffic will route from the remote office to a VPN device, travel securely over the Internet, and into the VPN device on the corporate network. Once on the corporate network the end user will have the potential to access any of the corporate services or servers. As shown below, Hacker Bob is thwarted once again and cannot read your sensitive data:

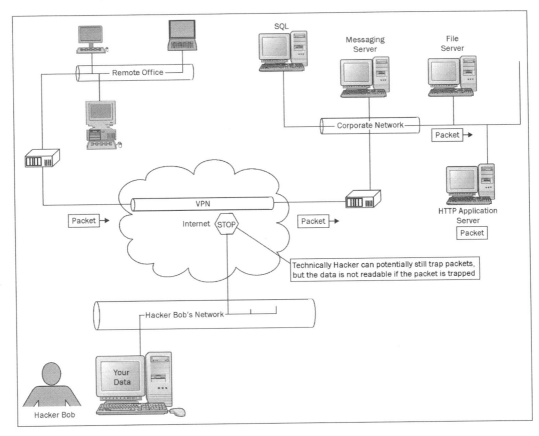

Now your problem is solved; your company is able to provide access to its corporate office computers from anywhere in the world. And the final result—Hacker Bob will be looking elsewhere to launch his evil plan.

VPN Examples

Let's look at some of the different protocols for creating secure VPNs over the Internet:

- **L2TP**: Layer-2 Tunneling Protocol
- **IPsec**: IP Security Protocol

L2TP or **Layer-2 Tunneling Protocol** is a combination of Microsoft's **Point-to-Point Tunneling Protocol (PPTP)** and the Cisco **Layer-2 Forwarding (L2F)**. L2TP is a network protocol and it can send encapsulated packets over networks like IP, X.25, Frame Relay, **Multiprotocol Label Switching (MPLS)**, or **Asynchronous Transfer Mode (ATM)**.

IPsec will encrypt all outgoing data and decrypt all incoming data so that you can use a public network, like the Internet, as a transportation media. IPsec VPNs normally utilize protocols at Layer 3 of the OSI Model. This is effectuated by using two different techniques:

- Authentication Header (AH)
- Encapsulating Security Payload (ESP)

The **Authentication Header** provides two-way device authentication, which can be implemented in hardware or software, and in many cases provide user authentication via a standard set of credentials—user ID and password. You may also see implementations using a token, or an X.509 user certificate.

The **Encapsulating Security Payload** protocol provides the data encryption. Most implementations support algorithms such as **DES (Data Encryption Standard)**, **3DES (Triple Data Encryption Standard)**, or **AES (Advanced Encryption Standard)**. In its most basic configuration, IPsec will implement a handshake that requires each end point to exchange keys and then agree on security policies.

IPsec

IPsec can support two encryption modes:

- **Transport**: encrypts the data portion of each packet, but leaves the header unencrypted. The original routing information in the packet is not protected from being viewed by unauthorized parties.
- **Tunnel**: encrypts both the header and the data. The original routing data is encrypted, and an additional set of routing information is added to the packet to be used for routing between the two endpoints.

IPsec supports a protocol known as the **Internet Security Association and Key Management Protocol/Oakley (ISAKMP/Oakley)**. This protocol allows the receiver to obtain a public key and authenticate the sender using digital certificates. The basic process of a key-based cryptography system provides a method of exchanging one key of a key pair. Once the keys are exchanged, the traffic can be encrypted. IPsec is described in many RFCs, including 2401, 2406, 2407, 2408, and 2409. Also see RFC 3193 for securing L2TP using IPsec.

The downside to a client-based VPN (such as those using IPSEC or L2TP) is that you need to configure and/or install some type of software. Yes, there is code that is built into Windows for a VPN, but you still need to configure the client. In some cases you may even need to install a client certificate. In addition, personal firewalls, anti-virus software, and other security technologies may be necessary. The basic configuration for an IPsec VPN is a central site hub device and a remote client computer. Once the connection has been established then a tunnel is created over the network (private or pubic). This encrypted tunnel will secure the communication between the end points, and once again our best buddy Hacker Bob is not able to read our communications.

Secure VPNs

VPNC (Virtual Private Network Consortium) supports three protocols for secure VPN (L2TP, IPsec, and SSL/TLS) and another two protocols for trusted VPNs (MPLS and Transport of layer 2 frames over MPLS). For securing L2TP using IPsec (see http://www.vpnc.org/rfc3193).

SSL VPN

Another option that is available to secure traffic on the Internet is **Secure Socket Layer (SSL)**. SSL is a protocol that provides encryption for network-based traffic. SSL is a network protocol with responsibility for the management of a secure, encrypted, communication channel between a server and a client. SSL is implemented in the major Web browsers such as Internet Explorer, Netscape, and Firefox. One of the most basic functions of SSL is message privacy. SSL can encrypt a session between a client and a server so that applications can exchange and authenticate user names and passwords without exposing them to eavesdroppers. SSL will block Hacker Bob's attempts to read our data by scrambling it.

One of the most powerful features of SSL is the ability for the client and server to prove their identities by exchanging certificates. All traffic between the SSL server and SSL client is encrypted using a shared key and a negotiated encryption algorithm. This is all effectuated during the SSL handshake, which occurs at session initialization. Another feature of SSL protocol is that SSL will ensure that messages between the sender system and receiving system have not been tampered with during the transmission. The result is that SSL provides a secure channel between a client and a server. SSL was basically designed to make the security process transparent to the end user. Normally a user would follow a URL to a page that connects to an SSL-enabled server (see RFC1738— http://ds.internic.net/rfc/rfc1738.txt). The SSL-enabled server would accept connect requests on TCP port 443 (which is the default port for SSL). When it connects to port 443 the handshake process will establish the SSL session.

Several years ago there was a creative advertisement showing one person walking down the street eating chocolate and another person walking down the street eating peanut butter: they run into each other and now we have a product that comprises chocolate and peanut butter together. This is exactly what happened with the SSL VPN.

This combination of SSL and VPN provides us with the following benefits:

- This combination of SSL encryption and proxy technologies can provide very simple access to Web and corporate applications.

- The marriage of technologies can provide client and server authentication with data encryption between each party.

- Overall, it can be easier to set up an SSL VPN than to set up and manage an IPsec VPN.

More benefits of SSL VPN technology will be discussed in the next chapter.

In some respects, the SSL VPN implementation will be similar to that of IPsec. SSL VPNs will also require some type of a hub device. Also the client will require some type of communication software, namely an SSL-enabled web browser. As most computers have an SSL-enabled browser that includes *root* SSL certificates from certified public Certificate Authorities (CA), by default SSL VPN access is available from the client. Additional client software can be downloaded automatically during SSL VPN sessions (typically this software is in the form of an applet plug-in). The central hub device and the software client will encrypt the data over an IP network. This process of encryption will make the data unreadable to Hacker Bob.

> A full discussion of public and private CA can be found in *The Internet Security Guidebook: From Planning to Deployment* available at:
> `http://www.amazon.com/exec/obidos/tg/detail/-/0122374711/102-0386261-4698507?v=glance`.

IPsec Vs. SSL VPN

Most IPsec VPNs will use custom software at each of the end points—the hub device and client. If you think about this for a bit then you will see that this process provides a high level of security. Each end point requires some type of setup steps, potentially adding more human intervention into the process.

The SSL VPN normally will not require any special client software. The overall security is the same as that of the IPsec solution. As far as setup goes, if the browser is up-to-date then the process is automatic.

Both IPsec and SSL VPNs can provide enterprise-level secure remote access. Both these technologies support a range of user authentication methods, including X.509 certificates. IPsec overall is more vulnerable to attack, unless certificates are used. SSL Web servers always authenticate with digital certificates, even in the one-way based authentication that native SSL uses. SSL will determine if the target server is certified by any of the CAs. SSL provides better flexibility in cases where trust is limited or where it is difficult (or unwise) to install user certificates (for example, on public computers)

Trusted Networks

A Trusted Network of a company is a network that the company uses to conduct its internal business. In many cases, the Trusted Network is by default defined in the organization as 'Secure'. The Trusted Network typically supports the backend systems, internal-only intranet web pages, data processing, messaging, and in some cases, internal instant messaging. In many companies the Trusted Network is allowed to interact between systems directly, without encryption. The problem with the definition above is that many assumptions are being made at these companies. A Trusted Network is not always a secure network. In fact, in many cases the Trusted Network cannot be trusted. The reason is that an internal network comprises many different networks. These include new acquisitions, old acquisitions, international access points, and even several access points to the outside world. A common practice is to define the Trusted Network as the network that internal employees use when at the office or via a secure controlled dial-in mechanism. A single access point is established to the outside world via a mechanism called the **Demilitarized Zone (DMZ)**.

The DMZ

The DMZ is an isolated network placed as a buffer area between a company's Trusted Network and the Non-trusted Network. The Internet is always defined as untrusted. By design, the DMZ prevents outside users from gaining direct access to the Trusted Network. The following figure shows a generic DMZ:

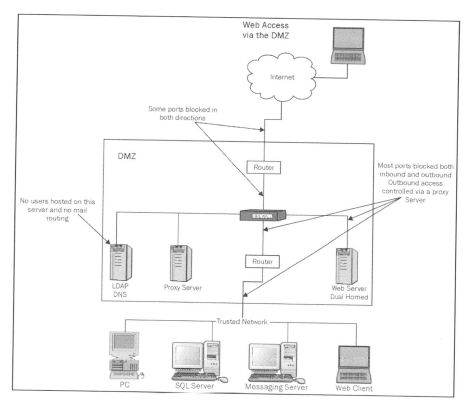

Most DMZs are configured via a set of rules that are controlled by the Policies and then implemented via the Procedures for your organization. One of the most common rules is that a single port number (like 80) cannot traverse the DMZ. So if you are attempting to access an application on a DMZ via HTTP on port 80, then that port cannot terminate into the trusted network via the DMZ. This is what the DMZ does; it keeps untrusted traffic from entering the Trusted Network. It is the job of the DMZ to filter the traffic and limit access to the Trusted Network via filtering and authentication, and even to completely block traffic if needed. Here are a few examples of what the DMZ can do:

- Block port scans of your Trusted Network
- Block access to the Trusted Network via a single TCP port
- Block **Denial** of **Service Attacks (DoS)** from your trusted network
- Scan email messages for virus, content, and size
- Block passive eavesdropping/packet sniffing

SSL VPN Scenarios

So, how does SSL VPN fit into corporate network infrastructure? Below are a couple of examples of SSL VPN access.

- SSL VPN access to selected devices via the use of an SSL VPN hub (access from the Internet)
- SSL VPN access to a *special network* that uses an SSP VPN hub sitting between the trusted network and the special network

SSL VPN—Hubs

One of the key security elements of a DMZ is the ability to terminate the IP connection at various points in the DMZ and the trusted network. The example below shows a client connection on the Internet (untrusted) to an SSL VPN hub on a trusted network.

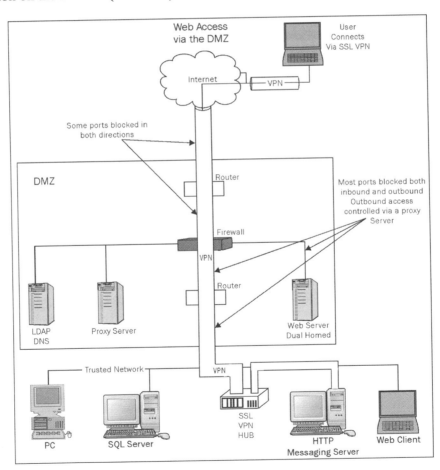

The traffic is routed into the DMZ, and then is terminated at the router. The IP address is now translated to a DMZ IP address, for example 10.10.10.10. The DMZ can then provide some authentication and allow the traffic to route to the trusted side of the DMZ. At this point the IP address can be translated to another IP address, like 192.168.10.12. The packets are then routed to the SSL VPN device (hub).

The SSL VPN will execute additional checks on the traffic. If all tests are passed then, based on a set of rules and authentication, the traffic could be routed to the HTTP messaging server. In this example you could have a CxO (CEO, CIO, CTO, etc.) on vacation, checking out the Lion King playing on 42nd street. Before sitting down, the CxOwalks into the Internet Café next door and checks his or her email. Now the CxO can feel secure that Hacker Bob will not be able to read those important corporate emails.

Network architectures used to support SSL VPN access from the Internet will be discussed in detail in Chapter 4.

SSL VPN—Private Network

Many large enterprise companies will have private networks. These private networks can span not only just their home country, but can also span the globe. In many cases, these private networks will interconnect via several Internet Service Providers (ISPs). Also some companies will not only have a private network at their local office, but will also have a **Point of Presence (POP)** to the Internet. This can add additional challenges to keeping the private network secure; each POP is an opportunity for Hacker Bob to enter the network. Additionally, not all corporate employees and contractors are necessarily honest; some may also pose a threat to internal resources. As a result, large companies often regard their trusted private network as untrusted. The risk is that there can be unauthorized access into the private network at several points—not only from the POPs, but also from the ISP. The example below shows where SSL and/or SSL VPNs can be used to provide secure access where the network is NOT trusted:

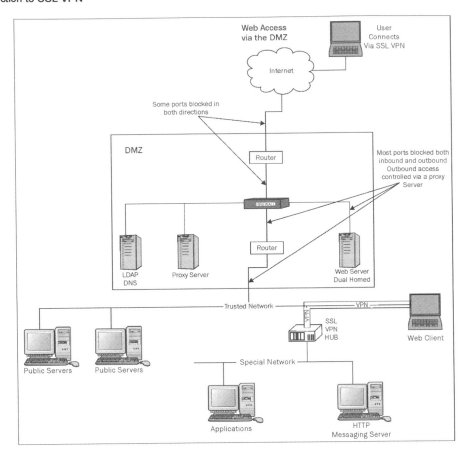

In the above example, the end user is hosted on the corporate trusted network. The end user may want to access a web page, messaging, or even their file server. Traffic will originate at the end user's computer and will be routed via the trusted network basic address, for example, 192.168.10.22. Packets are terminated in the SSL VPN hub; at this point the data is then routed to each service. Now, a worldwide organization can determine that its data transfers are secure, and not readable by bad old Hacker Bob.

Summary

This chapter served as an introduction to understanding the world of SSL VPN. We discussed TCP/IP networking, the Internet, how VPNs keep communications secure over insecure networks, and looked at different VPN technologies.

The remainder of this book discusses the details of SSL VPN—what it is, how it works, how to secure it, why it makes sense business wise, and more.

2

SSL VPN: The Business Case

As alluded to in Chapter 1, the need to provide remote access to important electronic resources such as applications, files, and databases is not new. For several decades, businesses, governments, and organizations have realized that significant benefits could be achieved by delivering such access to various parties. These benefits include:

- **Improving work force productivity**:
    - ○ Employees and contractors can perform tasks even when not physically present in their usual work facilities.

    - ○ People are often willing to work more hours if they are permitted to work from home.

    - ○ Managers and administrators can respond faster to emergency conditions and may be willing to respond to less-critical events immediately rather than applying an "it can wait until tomorrow" attitude as they would if they had to return to work after retiring home at the conclusion of normal business hours.

- **Lowering costs**:
    - ○ Increased self-service capabilities for conducting business with outside parties such as suppliers and customers leads to lowers costs

    - ○ In some business environments in which employees can work remotely on a regular basis (e.g., IT consulting), an organization that offers remote access can maintain less office space (and save money). Workspaces can be assigned to those employees actually in the facility on a particular day (for example, by implementing a 'hoteling' scheme).

    - ○ Increased self-service capabilities for suppliers improve their efficiency, yielding better-negotiated service/product rates.

    - ○ If remote access is used as part of business-continuity strategy, fewer seats may be necessary at disaster-recovery/business-continuity facilities than if all workers must work at the secondary site.

Hoteling refers to an office management technique that involves allocating office space to a particular individual for the time he or she actually plans to be in the office. Typically, workers notify an administrator (or use an automated reservation system to specify) as to which dates they plan to be in the office, and space is allocated to them for that time period.

Since some percentage of users are not in the office on any given day, the organization need not incur the costs of renting and maintaining enough space to simultaneously accommodate the workspace requirements of every employee.

- **Increases top-line revenue**:
  - o Employees who bill customers for their time (for example, attorneys, accountants, consultants) may generate more billable hours if they can work some of those hours from home.
  - o Increased self-service capabilities for prospects and customers will attract new customers.

- **Assurance of business continuity**:
  - o Users can work remotely in case of a disaster.
  - o Even non-critical employees who may not have workspaces at a recovery facility can be productive.

SSL VPN: A Historical Background

To fully understand the business value of SSL VPN (and why it delivers certain benefits better than alternative technologies) it is wise to understand what factors influence the value of a remote access solution in general as well as how SSL VPN figures into the overall picture and history of remote computing.

We begin with a discussion of how and why SSL VPN came to be and the way it evolved. Early remote access was typically achieved using one of two methods: **Direct modem-based dial up** or **leased lines**.

1. **Direct modem-based dial-up**: Users would connect to an organization by dialing (using a modem connected to their computers) a phone number belonging to the host office. Dialing this number connected the user to a modem bank at the site to which he wanted to connect. This type of access allowed users to connect from anywhere—as long as the user had access to a computer and modem (and perhaps some special software installed on the

computer as well), and had access to a phone line. This is illustrated in the following figure:

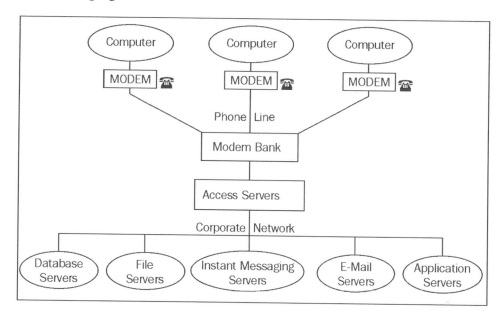

Dial up offered the remote access that organizations wanted, and was certainly a wonderful technology in its day, but with the dawn and maturation of the Internet age, its days appear numbered as:

○ **It is expensive**: Modem pools need to be purchased and maintained, numerous phone lines to be leased, and long-distance telephone charges are incurred for connections made by remote users. Remote users are often working in hotel rooms from which the cost of placing long distance calls can be quite exorbitant.

○ **Connection speeds are pitifully slow**: The fastest modem connections offer communications speeds of under 56-kilobits per second. Today, significant percentages of businesspeople have DSL or Cable connections to the Internet at home (or in hotels). Such connections provide up to 200 times the maximum speed of dial up connections. Furthermore, media-rich business activities—those involving the transfer to images, voice, or video or even sending large presentations or spreadsheets—can render dial-up's performance unacceptable to most users.

○ **Fiscal inefficiency**: In many environments, most phone lines and modems in the modem bank remain idle most of the time, but during peak usage periods (e.g., in an emergency when users cannot get to their offices), all of the modems/lines may be tied up, making remote access unavailable for some users (a self-initiated Denial-of-Service condition).

- o **Security**: Dial up modem pools are an easy target for low-tech Denial of Service attacks—all that the hackers need to do is tie up the phone lines by dialing the modems.

- o **Access requires that the user have an analog dial up line**: Making remote access impossible for many users. For example, consultants working on-site at customer sites often do not have a modem line available to them.

2. **Leased lines**: **Leased lines** refer to private digital connections between two or more locations (In reality these lines may be over shared trunks but the bandwidth allocated is for use only by the leaser and only for connections between the two pre-determined endpoints.). Such lines have been used for secure site-to-site connectivity—for example, connecting two remote offices together on a WAN—for quite some time. But with the appearance of more modern technologies, the cost of leasing such lines is growing increasingly unattractive especially when compared with VPN connections over the Internet (which we will discuss in the next section).

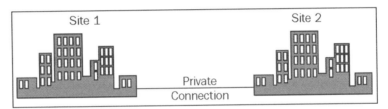

Leased lines also provide connectivity only between two pre-determined endpoints. So they are not usable for remote access if a user has to travel to more than one remote location. They are rarely used for user-to-site connections (i.e. for users to gain remote access); with some notable exceptions where there is a significant need for a particular user to be able to access specific functions from specific locations, and the security is absolutely critical.

Many site-to-site connections formerly made over private leased lines are being made over various forms of VPN connections. (Of course, some sensitive situations mandate that private lines still be used.)

With the coming of the Internet age, **IPsec VPN** (and some other similar remote access technologies) became a viable alternative to the two aforementioned options.

IPsec VPN and other similar technologies (IPsec was the most popular) leveraged the Internet to establish a private communications channel over the public Internet (this is described in more detail in Chapter 4). By leveraging the Internet, the cost of providing site-to-site connectivity was dramatically reduced (when compared with leased lines), and user-to-site remote access became possible at much higher speeds than before (compared to dial up connections).

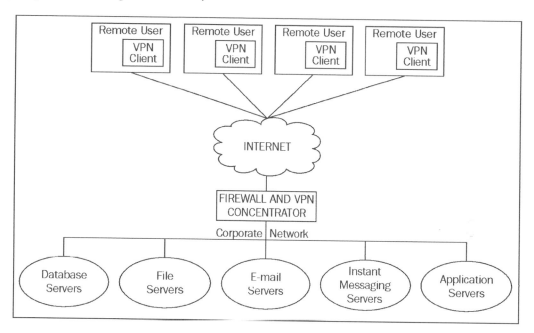

IPsec VPN, though, suffers from several drawbacks that are growing increasingly problematic with advances in technology:

1. IPsec effectively establishes the remote device as a node on the internal network. So it should only be used from computers that an organization would allow to be plugged into their network had the machines been located within the physical confines of their facilities. Corporate-governed (and other trusted) computers may be acceptable for IPsec VPN usage in this regard but all other computers may not meet such restrictions. Properly implementing an IPsec VPN, therefore, offers remote access only from a small number of computers; most Internet-connected devices are unfit to be used for remote access. As a result of restricting access to be only from secure computers, organizations are often forced to purchase laptop computers for people to use when working remotely—even if these folks already have home computers. This translates into both the cost of purchasing and maintaining extra machines, as well as the cost differential between buying desktops and laptops—laptops are more expensive than comparable desktops.

2. As mentioned in Chapter 1, IPsec VPNs typically require that users run special software on any client device used to access the network. The cost of purchasing, installing, and maintaining such software adds up quickly, especially since we are talking about maintaining software on machines that are often located in remote locations. Furthermore—because IPsec established network-type connectivity between corporate networks and remote users—antivirus software, anti-spam software, and anti-spyware software required on any computer connected to the corporate network inside an office must be installed and maintained on remote machines used for access. Ensuring that updated signature databases are installed on remote machines can be difficult and expensive. Sometimes third-party products are used to ensure that computers used for access have proper software configurations and updates. This may simplify the process of managing the remote devices but adds additional cost. Additionally, personal firewalls and other security tools must be implemented to ensure that the remote node does not become a gateway for other machines to inappropriately enter the enterprise's infrastructure. All of these technologies, required on machines used with IPsec VPNs, add further costs that can grow dramatically with time and a growing user population.

3. Some Internet providers block IPsec traffic from residential customers, or at least make it difficult for home users to configure their computers to use IPsec VPNs. In environments in which this limitation is present, IPsec is clearly not a good mechanism for offering users remote access.

SSL VPN entered the marketplace as a technology intended to deliver the benefits that users derive from IPsec VPN (and more) but without many of the drawbacks. It leverages web browsers to provide access to enterprise applications, systems, files, and other resources from essentially any Internet-connected web browser abandoning the long-standing model of requiring specialized client software to enable VPN remote access. It leveraged three developments in the market that enabled its emergence:

1. The rapid deployment of World Wide Web browsers and the fact that browsers are now available in an amazing number of locations worldwide (and even extra-terrestrially in the International Space Station!)

2. The fact that high speed Internet is growing increasingly common

3. The fact that many applications now offer web interfaces

Although SSL VPNs now support access to resources other than applications with web interfaces, early SSL VPNs typically were limited in this regard. Some offered access exclusively to web applications; others had limited capabilities to offer some degree of access to other resources.

The convergence of these factors created a situation in which remote access technologies could rely on the presence of a uniform client at all locations without having to install special client software. That client is, of course, the web browser. Since 2002, as both web browsers and SSL VPN technology improved, many new capabilities have been added to SSL VPNs (these will be discussed in the remaining chapters of the book).

SSL VPN technology was intended to address user-to-site access, not site-to-site connectivity. IPsec VPN is still the dominant technique for implementing secure site-to-site connectivity across the Internet.

Remote Access: Measuring Return-on-Investment

In general, the value of a solution designed to provide users with remote access to enterprise resources can be judged on four criteria:

1. **Who can gain remote access**: This includes factors such as:

    o   How many users can gain access in total?

    o   How many users can gain access simultaneously without severely degrading the performance?

    o   How complicated is the remote access technology? Will non-technical users be able to use it?

2. **Where can they access from**: This includes factors such as:

    o   From how many different types of machines can remote access be achieved?

    o   Are there any technical requirements at the endpoints (e.g., for special hardware or software) that would preclude access from specific types of locations or devices?

3. **What can be accessed**: This includes factors such as:

    o   How many different types of resources can be made available remotely using the particular remote-access technology?

    o   Are the systems fully available or just in limited form?

      o Will security policies cause access to be a problem?

   4. **What is the cost of providing such access**: This includes both:

      o The purchase, installation, and configuration of the remote access technology—i.e. the initial layout

      o The cost of maintaining and supporting the system—i.e. ongoing expenses

As we will see when we review the history of remote access technologies, SSL VPN excels in these areas when compared with earlier technologies.

So What Does SSL VPN Actually Give Me?

The following matrix illustrates how various remote-access technologies SSL VPN meet the value criteria discussed earlier in this chapter.

	Dial Up	Leased Lines	IPSEC VPN	SSL VPN
Who	Limited to users who have computers the organization will allow to be connected to its network	Typically only a very small number of special users for whom the cost can be justified (e.g., the CEO)	Only users with special computers with special software. Limited to users who have computers the organization will allow to be connected to its network	All users
From Where	From anywhere the user has access to a modem line	From one location—the endpoint of the leased line	From the special computers using any Internet connection	From essentially any Internet connected device
What	Only resources that are not bandwidth intensive	Most internal resources	Most internal resources	Most internal resources
Cost	High	Very high	High	Low

In short, it is clear from the above matrix that SSL VPN can deliver remote access to more people, in more locations, using more diverse devices than older technologies *and* at a lower cost. It enables organizations to deploy remote access to users who never before had remote access, and to replace older remote-access technologies with a less expensive and more efficient mechanism of delivering remote access.

> SSL VPN access may be limited—or may not work altogether—from some older web browsers. The number of obsolete browsers that do not support SSL remote access that are still in use, however, is not terribly great and continues to diminish. With time, this issue should essentially disappear.

Additionally, because SSL VPN allows access from anywhere, it can be incorporated as an integral strategy for use in business continuity plans. SSL VPNs can be used to allow users to continue performing their jobs in various situations including:

1. Users are cut off from their normal work facilities, but the facilities and communications lines remain live. This is common in cases of severely inclement weather, and occurs with relative frequency in metropolitan areas when transportation is limited due to transit strikes, protest demonstrations or rallies, emergency construction, or gatherings with high-profile attendees.

2. If the primary work facility is incapacitated but the organization has replicated systems (or otherwise recovered) to a remote site, SSL VPN allows users to work off the remote systems without having to travel to a distant location. This:

   o **Saves the organization money**: It needs to pay for fewer workspaces in the backup facility

   o **Allows more users to remain productive**: Seats in a backup facility are normally made available only to the employees performing the most critical and time-sensitive business functions

   o **Improves morale**: Employees are often unwilling (or at least extremely upset by the need) to leave their families immediately after a disaster or emergency—which is often when continuity plans are activated.

Summary

In this chapter we reviewed the business reasons for implementing remote access, looked at how and why SSL VPN emerged, and discussed how SSL VPN can provide great value to organizations searching for a remote access solution. We explained the unique qualities of SSL VPN technology that enable it to provide remote access to the following than was previously possible:

- more people
- working on a greater number of machines
- from more locations
- and at a lower cost

In the next chapter we will look at how SSL VPNs actually work—what is inside the slick-looking appliances.

3

How SSL VPNs Work

As described in Chapter 1, SSL VPN products allow users to establish secure remote-access sessions from virtually any Internet-connected web browser. Delivering the ability for people to access e-mail, critical information systems, files, and other network resources from virtually anywhere is not a trivial task. Despite often appearing to onlookers as simple devices, SSL VPNs employ complex and advanced technology.

At present, there are no official standards for SSL VPN technology (other than for SSL, HTTP, and other SSL VPN subcomponents). The few third-party SSL VPN 'certifiers' that exist, primarily examine features, not the internal mechanisms of delivering those features. With a highly competitive climate currently present in the SSL VPN market, vendors are also reluctant to disclose the details of the inner workings of their products. Yet, even without official information from each vendor, it is possible to understand SSL VPN technology. Every offering in the market faces similar challenges in providing web-based remote access. As a result, the basic technology utilized by SSL VPN products exhibits many common attributes across products. As such, in Chapter 2 we will explore the internal workings of SSL VPN technology not from the perspective of any particular offering, but rather from a generic approach.

There are many complex technologies utilized by SSL VPNs, many of which designers, administrators, and users of SSL VPNs need not be intimately familiar with in order to understand SSL VPN. The intention of this chapter is to provide the reader with an overview of how SSL VPN technology works and provide sufficient information about each component of SSL VPN technology. Enough information is provided to understand SSL VPN, though we will not cover every detail about every technology subcomponent.

Appliances Vs. Software

In today's market, security products such as SSL VPNs are often sold as *appliances*, a term used to connote 'black boxes' that function without requiring administrators to understand their internal workings. In theory, appliances thereby reduce the overhead costs of installing, configuring, and maintaining an IT system.

Although some isolation from the internal technology certainly exists when it comes to SSL VPN offerings in appliance form, most appliances consist of standard computers running SSL VPN software on (a hardened version of) a standard operating system. Therefore—from a security standpoint—there is no intrinsic advantage in implementing an SSL VPN with an appliance-based form factor over an SSL VPN product sold as software that can be installed on servers of the purchaser's choice.

> Other components may be present in SSL VPN appliances such as SSL Accelerators, Air Gap Switches, etc. These topics are covered in Chapter 4 and 5 of this book.

Practically speaking, however, appliances are typically shipped with their operating systems hardened, SSL VPN software installed, and rudimentary configuration options set. As a result, they reduce the amount of human error likely to occur during the process of installation and configuration, and ensure that no conflicts occur between hardening procedures and the SSL VPN software. In many situations, therefore, the appliance-based offering presents security-related advantages over software. Nonetheless, organizations with data-center standards dictate that preferred brands of servers may prefer a software-based product; this is especially true in situations in which administrators are already skilled in hardening systems.

The figures below show SSL VPN appliances from (left to right) Safenet, Juniper Networks, and Whale Communications:

Regardless of which physical option is selected for implementation, the underlying technology of SSL VPNs remains identical.

The SSL Protocol

As is obvious from the name SSL VPN, the **Secure Sockets Layer** protocol (**SSL**) is a key element of SSL VPN technology. As such, a basic understanding of SSL will help us understand the workings of SSL VPNs.

Background

Web pages are delivered using the **Hypertext Transfer Protocol (HTTP)**. HTTP in itself does not offer encryption or any other substantial protection of data transmitted between users and web servers. With the advent of the World Wide Web in the early 1990s and the goal of extending Web usage to actual business activity involving the transmission of confidential information over the Internet came the need to eliminate eavesdropping by unauthorized parties on web communications between computers over the Internet.

Several technologies were proposed to address this need—all of them utilizing encryption to protect sensitive data in transit. The protocol that quickly proved dominant and which ultimately became the standard for secure web communications was SSL.

SSL Version 1.0 was introduced in the Mosaic browser in 1994, and an enhanced version (SSL Version 2.0) was commercially offered later in the same year when the inventors of Mosaic formed a for-profit enterprise ultimately called Netscape Communications and released their Navigator web browser.

As is still the case, by looking at a web page's URL in those browsers a user could determine if a particular page was delivered over SSL-encrypted communications. SSL encrypted pages had the prefix https whereas non-encrypted pages used a prefix of http. (Today in addition to the change in the URL, most browsers display some icon indicating that the session is encrypted—a lock, a key, etc. This will be discussed in detail in Chapter 6.)

HTTPS is the web protocol that utilizes SSL to encrypt HTTP, and is used worldwide today for secure web communications. HTTPS should not be confused with S-HTTP, an alternative method for encrypting web communications. S-HTTP competed with HTTPS in the early days of secure web sessions, but was generally considered inferior to HTTPS for e-commerce use (as it did not encrypt some session information), and is no longer used.

S-HTTP is an extension to the HTTP protocol used to support sending data securely over the World Wide Web. S-HTTP is designed to send individual messages securely where as SSL is designed to establish a secure connection between two computers.

Today, servers typically provide regular web service (HTTP) on port 80, and SSL-encrypted web traffic (HTTPS) over port 443.

Overleaf is an HTTPS encrypted web page. Note the https at the start of the URL and the lock icon near the bottom right of the screenshot:

In 1995, Microsoft released its initial version of Internet Explorer, which was armed with its own encryption technology called **Private Communications Technology (PCT)**. PCT offered some advantages over SSL Version 2.0. However, shortly after Internet Explorer's release, Netscape released SSL Version 3.0, which rendered the Microsoft benefits over the pervious iteration of SSL irrelevant. SSL 3.0 permanently delivered the market for secure Web communications into the hands of the SSL proponents.

In 1996, as the relevance of the World-Wide Web as a respectable mainstream business channel and communications mechanism became assured, and as SSL emerged as an effectively unchallenged de facto standard, the **Internet Engineering Task Force (IETF)** began formal standardization of the SSL protocol. In 1999, it completed its work and established SSL as the official standard for secure Web communications under the name **Transport Layer Security (TLS)**.

Besides protecting data through encryption, SSL uses hashing to ensure that the contents of a communications session are not modified between the time one computer sends a message and the time the recipient reads it.

A **hash value** is a number generated from a string of text by applying some mathematical algorithm. The hash result is typically substantially smaller than the text itself, and is generated by a formula in such a way that it is extremely unlikely that some other source text will produce the same hash value. A **hash formula** is a one-way function—that is, it is infeasible to reverse the process to determine the original text. **Hashing** is the act of applying a hash formula to a string of text to obtain a hash value.

It is interesting to note that despite its success in the arena of web encryption, in another area the SSL has proven a miserable failure. A second goal of SSL was to prevent counterfeit websites from stealing user data by impersonating valid websites with which people want to transact business. Although SSL technology does offer a sound method for users to verify server identities, the technical sophistication required in order to do so has rendered this capability impractical for mass acceptance. It is precisely after SSL has matured, been adopted as an official standard, and deployed ubiquitously and universally, that the problem of counterfeit websites has become an epidemic. The **phishing** type of crime in which users are tricked into surrendering confidential information to mischievous parties impersonating valid businesses was virtually unheard of before SSL's adoption. Phishing is believed to be costing millions of dollars in fraud-type damage every month. At present, this deficiency in SSL poses a far greater risk to online commercial activity than it does to SSL VPN implementations.

SSL also offers mechanisms for authenticating clients. By presenting client certificates users can prove their identity to a server. Although this capability of SSL is rarely used, it has special significance in the world of SSL VPNs as it allows SSL VPN servers to identify client machines of different trust levels. This is discussed in detail in Chapter 4.

Goals of SSL

1. Confidentiality of communications (primary use)

2. Integrity of Data (primary use—not noticed by users)

3. Authentication of Server (relies on user to be technically well informed)

4. Authentication of Client (rarely used, but has applications for SSL VPN)

Overview of SSL Technology

SSL uses cryptographic algorithms to encrypt data so that only the two computers that are supposed to be able to read a message can actually understand it. This is known as protecting data confidentiality. SSL supports different encryption algorithms; the algorithms that are available for a particular encrypted session vary based on SSL version, company policies, and governmental restrictions.

There are two types of cryptography used within each SSL session, **Symmetric** and **Asymmetric**. While symmetric encryption is used for encrypting all the communications within an SSL session, an asymmetric algorithm is used to share the symmetric session key securely between the user and the SSL VPN.

There are entire books written on symmetric and asymmetric cryptography, but all that we need to understand are the basics. One good book for the beginner is *Cryptography for Dummies* by Chey Cobb (ISBN 0-7645-4188-9).

Symmetric Cryptography: Data Confidentiality

Symmetric algorithms use the same key for encryption and decryption and, therefore, both parties in a conversation must share a common key as shown in the following figure. Processing symmetric cryptography requires fewer CPU cycles than processing asymmetric. However, symmetric cryptography suffers from one major drawback—how does one party securely share the secret key with the other party if they are separated by the insecure Internet?

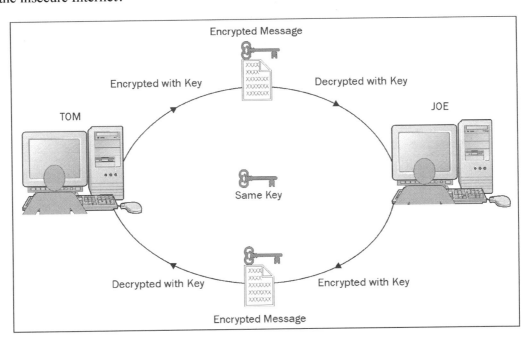

A **key** is a piece of data (usually a large number) that is fed to a cryptographic algorithm in order to encrypt plaintext into ciphertext or to decrypt ciphertext into plaintext. Utilizing the same algorithms with different keys will produce different results.

Asymmetric Cryptography: Data Confidentiality

Asymmetric cryptography addresses the problem of key exchange. It uses key pairs; one key in a pair is called a **public key** and another is called a **private key**. The public key is not secret as it is shared with the public. The private key, on the other hand, remains private and only its owner should ever have access to it. Data encrypted with one in key in a key pair can only be decrypted with the corresponding key in the pair. It cannot be decrypted with the same key with which it was encrypted. For example, when Tom wants to send a message to Joe that only Joe should be able to read, Tom encrypts the message with Joe's public key. Since the message can be decrypted only with Joe's private key, and only Joe possesses that key, only Joe can read the message. Likewise, when Joe responds to Tom, he encrypts his message with Tom's public key. As the only keys that need to be shared in an asymmetric model are public keys, and public keys are not secret, asymmetric cryptography does not suffer from an issue of key sharing. Public keys can easily be transmitted over the Internet as illustrated by the following figure:

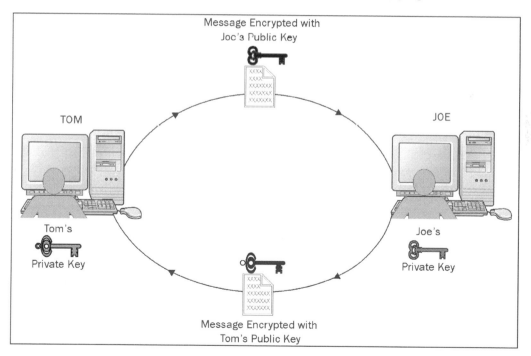

However, asymmetric cryptography is extremely processor intensive and not practical for encrypting large amounts of data. It cannot be used to encrypt an entire SSL session. Nevertheless, it is ideal for use as a mechanism to transfer symmetric keys securely across an insecure network, and it is exactly for this purpose that SSL uses it. So SSL uses asymmetric cryptography to share a secret key between the remote user and a server, and then uses that key to perform symmetric encryption/decryption on the data sent during the SSL session as shown overleaf:

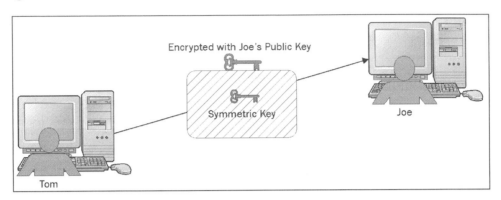

Asymmetric Cryptography: Server Authentication

Besides encryption, asymmetric cryptography also provides the ability to sign messages. If a user encrypts a message with his or her own private key, any user who decrypts the message by using the sender's public key is assured that the sender was actually the party who sent the message. No one else would have been able to generate a message that can be decrypted with that public key as only the party who is in possession of the corresponding private key could possibly have encrypted the message.

SSL Certificates are a mechanism by which a web server can prove to users that the public key that it offers to them for use with SSL is in fact, the public key of the organization with which the user intends to communicate. A trusted third-party signs the certificate thereby assuring users that the public key contained within the certificate belongs to the organization whose name appears in the certificate. Upon receiving a certificate from ABC Company, a user can know for sure that the key within the certificate is ABC's key and it is safe to use such a key to encrypt communications related to establishment of a session key. This allows the user to know that he or she is speaking with ABC Company and not some imposter. An SSL certificate is the means by which web servers transmit their public keys to users at the beginning of an SSL session.

As stated previously, despite the server-authentication capabilities of SSL, phishing-type fraud has reached epidemic levels. The technical expertise required to appreciate SSL's anti-impersonation capabilities properly has severely limited its usefulness in the real world. During the establishment of an SSL-protected communication session, the user's computer will warn the user if a certificate is expired, not properly signed, untrusted, or does not match the server or domain from which it was received. Yet, most users do not understand warnings related to SSL certificates, and simply click OK or Accept when presented with messages about certificate problems.

Asymmetric Cryptography: Client Authentication

As mentioned previously, SSL provides for authentication of clients to servers through the use of certificates. Clients present a certificate to the server to prove their identity. Although implementations of such technology are rare, it has special significance in the world of SSL VPNs as it allows SSL VPN servers to identify client machines of different trust levels. This is discussed in detail in Chapter 3.

Key Size

At present, SSL encryption is normally utilized with session keys consisting of 128 random bits. With today's computers it is impractical to use brute-force techniques to decrypt data encrypted using keys of such a size. In earlier years, in order to meet US Export restrictions, SSL was commonly used with keys of 40 bits. But today, 40-bit keys do not provide sufficient security against brute force decryption attacks and so cannot be considered appropriate for encryption of sensitive material.

Establishing Secure Tunnels Using SSL

Now that we understand what SSL is and how it works, let us discuss how SSL allows us to create tunnels.

Secure Tunnels

A secure *tunnel* between computers can best be understood as a secure channel of communication between two machines that have an insecure environment between them. The communications tunnel is like a tunnel under a river that allows automobiles to travel from point A on one side of the river to point B on the other side and prevents environmental elements like water from interfering with the traffic as shown in the following diagram:

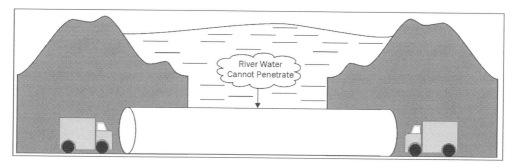

The communications tunnel allows communications between two computers over public networks securely so that other computers on those networks cannot access the communications between the two machines.

However, unlike the example of the tunnel under the river, network tunneling does not employ a physical barrier between the two computers communicating and other machines. Rather, computer-related tunneling involves encrypting all communications between the two computers so that even if another computer were to receive the communications, it would not be able to decipher the contents of the actual message between the machines as shown below:

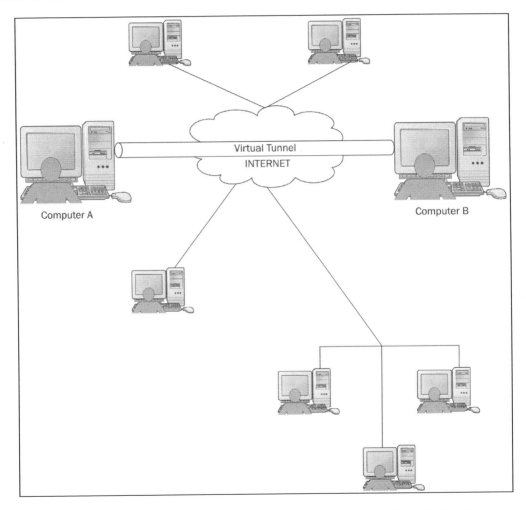

Tunneling is not a novel concept introduced with SSL VPN technology. It has been used in numerous technology implementations in the past, the most well known probably being **Internet Protocol Security (IPSec)** VPN (as described in chapter 1).

IPSec is an alternative network-level protocol to IP. It utilizes encryption to ensure that all datagrams sent on a network are unreadable by all machines on the network other than the sender and intended recipient. IPSec is not commonly used for general Internet communications, but is often used for VPN connections.

An encrypted tunnel between two computers over an insecure network such as the Internet is often known as a **Virtual Private Network**, since establishing such a tunnel connects these two computers in a fashion that resembles a private network connection. They can communicate without any other machine being able to intercept their communications. Although not immune to sniffing traffic as on a dedicated private line, VPN over the Internet has been deemed reliable and has become an accepted standard of communications in today's business world.

Sniffing refers to setting a computer's Network Interface card into 'promiscuous mode' in which it listens to all traffic on the network wire and reads in all data being transmitted—even those packets not intended for it to receive. Unless data is properly encrypted during communications, hackers can obtain the data by sniffing the network on which the data is traveling.

SSL VPNs create secure tunnels by performing two functions:

- Requiring authentication from users before allowing access so that only authorized parties can establish tunnels
- Encrypting all data transmitted to and from the user by implementing the actual tunnel using SSL

The process of establishing an SSL tunnel requires exchange of different configuration information between the computers on either end of the connection. The technical details related to communication and encryption protocols, key exchange, and so on are beyond the scope of this book. However, to understand SSL VPN technology, we should understand a little about the SSL protocol and SSL VPN's place within the OSI Model.

If you would like to learn more about the details of SSL Key Exchange please consult RFC 2246 available on the Internet Engineering Task Force website at `http://www.ietf.org/rfc/rfc2246.txt?number=2246`.

OSI Network Model

In 1984, Open Systems Interconnect, a group dedicated to providing international standards, released an abstract framework for classifying technologies involved in inter-computer communications (the model is described in detail in Chapter 1).

It consists of seven layers (or levels):

- **Level 7**: Application Layer
- **Level 6**: Presentation Layer
- **Level 5**: Session Layer
- **Level 4**: Transport Layer
- **Level 3**: Network Layer
- **Level 2**: Data Link Layer
- **Level 1**: Physical Layer

Historically, VPN tunneling was typically performed at the Network Layer or lower (e.g., IPSec, which operates at the Network Layer). Remote access was achieved by establishing encrypted network connectivity between a remote node and the internal network, making the remoteness of the connection invisible to all layers above Layer 4. Applications functioned identically when users were in the office and when they were remote, except that when the requests percolated down to the network level, they were relayed over the appropriate network connection for the user's specific location. Sometimes the connection was local and sometimes it involved tunneling back over the Internet. As discussed in Chapters 1 and 2, establishing such connections required the installation and configuration of complicated client software on users' computers. This client software managed the network-level tunneling.

SSL VPNs work differently. They establish connectivity using SSL, which functions at Levels 4-5. They also encapsulate information at Levels 6-7 and communicate at the highest levels in the OSI model. Today, some SSL VPNs are also able to tunnel network-level information over SSL, making SSL the most versatile remote access VPN technology available.

It is important to realize that SSL is not strictly a web protocol. It functions at the session and transport layers of the OSI model and can establish encrypted communication tunnels for various application-level protocols that may sit above it. For example, although SSL-encrypted web communication (HTTPS) is clearly the most common application of SSL, SSL encrypted POP3 and FTP are utilized in many environments. It is possible to use SSL to encrypt effectively any application-level protocol.

Application-Level Communications

So why don't SSL VPNs simply use SSL to tunnel network-level communications as IPSec does and not worry about the higher levels?

One of the major benefits of SSL VPN is the ability to access resources from any computer or even handheld device, at any location. This stems from the fact that communications can occur at the application level and is true for two reasons:

- Technical limitations of many devices prevent the establishment of network-level communications over SSL, but allow application-level access from a web browser.

- Security considerations and policies normally prohibit attaching Internet kiosks and borrowed computers as nodes on your corporate network.

Establishing connectivity at higher levels in the OSI Model, however, involves some costs and drawbacks. Strong standards for application-level communications do not exist as they do for TCP, UDP, IP, IPSec, and other networking and transport-level communications protocols. Individual applications do not conform to a universal language, specification, or format—a situation that significantly complicates managing communications to and from varied back-end applications.

The difference between application-level communications and network-level communications has a profound impact on security, and, this difference will be discussed in detail when we cover security issues in Chapter 4.

Reverse Proxy Technology

The most basic function of an SSL VPN is its ability to receive user requests and relay them to internal servers. This gateway-type function is called **reverse proxying**.

Technically speaking, a reverse proxy server is a computer that sits between an internal web server and the Internet and appears to external clients as if it were the true web server. External users address the reverse proxy thinking that it is servicing their requests, when in reality it simply relays their requests to a different server usually situated on the internal network. Responses work in a similar manner—the true server responds to the reverse proxy, which in turn relays the response to the user. Reverse proxies are often deployed as part of load-balancing schemes, as part of a layered security strategy, or simply to hide real servers from users for security reasons.

Reverse proxies, as seen in the diagram overleaf, serve as entry points into an organization's web infrastructure.

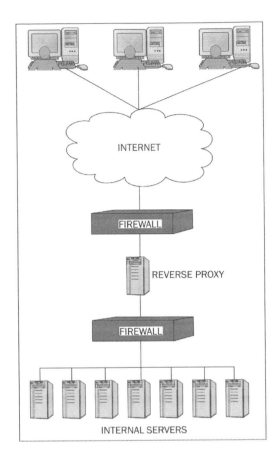

Web reverse proxies are certainly appropriate technologies for improving the security of Internet-accessible web-based systems and for simplifying load-balancing scenarios. However, they lack the ability to deliver many remote-access requirements. They cannot encapsulate client/server network traffic over SSL, cannot transform many internal applications to be Internet accessible, do not provide secure access to file systems, and do not offer a remote-access-oriented user interface. That is where SSL VPN technology comes in.

SSL Remote Access: Reverse Proxy Technology Plus

While advancements in SSL VPN have led to products sporting many other capabilities, at their core (and since the inception of SSL VPN technology) many SSL VPN servers utilize reverse-proxy-like technology to accept Web-based user requests and transmit them to internal resources. Of course, today's SSL VPNs add significant additional functionality to those reverse-proxy-type functions.

So, what does an SSL VPN offer in addition to standard reverse proxy functionality and why must it be added?

The primary technical enhancements, all of which are extremely significant when it comes to providing remote access, are:

- **Ability to allow both web and non-web applications to utilize the SSL tunnel for communication**: A simple Web reverse proxy allows access to only Web-based applications, but for SSL VPN technology to provide a viable remote access solution, other types of applications must also be made remotely available.

- **Ability to offer remote access to files, printers, and other resources**: Reverse proxies do not deliver such access.

- **Ability to transform intranet applications to be accessible via the Internet**: Some Web-based applications simply will not work through a reverse proxy, and an SSL VPN must be able to make them work remotely.

- **Ability to deliver a remote-access-oriented user experience**: Reverse proxies typically proxy requests without providing user interface enhancements to the applications that they are proxying

- **Ability to connect a remote device to a network** (i.e. deliver a network connection) **over SSL**

SSL VPN also adds all sorts of security functionality related to remote access, to which we dedicate an entire chapter (Chapter 4) in this book.

The aforementioned four items allow SSL VPN technology to deliver significantly more remote-access functionality; understanding them is to understand how SSL VPNs work. As such, we explore each of these four items in detail in the following sections.

Non-Web Traffic over SSL

As was stated earlier, one of the most significant improvements of SSL VPNs over reverse proxies is the ability to tunnel non-web traffic over SSL. Non-web applications often rely on proprietary client software and that software may communicate with servers on ports other than web ports. In fact, the software may dynamically choose ports using different ports for communication during each session. Reverse proxies, which typically relay data on ports 443 (HTTPS) and 80 (HTTP), cannot handle such communications, which are obviously a necessary ingredient of any viable remote-access solution.

So how does an SSL VPN allow such communications to occur over one single SSL port?

Although the various SSL VPN products do not utilize a uniform approach to address this challenge, several types of methods are becoming de facto standards:

- **Forwarding of Traffic sent to specific Ports**: The SSL VPN sends code to the user's machine that enables it to listen for requests to specific addresses and ports, and when such requests are made, it intercepts them. It then transfers the contents of the requests to the SSL VPN server via the SSL VPN tunnel, after which the SSL VPN server resends the requests to the actual destination on the internal network.

- **Transmission of data over native ports**: Effectively, the SSL VPN does not encapsulate application communications. Instead it dynamically opens ports in the firewall for communications from the client's specific IP access to its own address. Allowing such communications can be done without downloading any code to the client machine. The machine simply communicates to the server over the port native to that type of communication. Although this may be the simplest method to implement, it poses serious security risks and is usually not a viable option. It also involves the use of communications outside of SSL and deviates from the standard understanding of SSL VPN.

- **Utilization of operating-system components that allow redirection of traffic over the SSL VPN**: Today's robust operating systems provide various network-related hooks that can be utilized to redirect communications. For example, in a Windows environment the **NSP (Name Space Provider)** and **LSP (Layered Service Provider)** can be leveraged to redefine destinations for specific communications. Using such an approach to tunneling requires much more work on the part of the SSL VPN vendor than establishing network connectivity over SSL. At the same time it offers the ability to provide more granular controls over communications and better security.

- **Utilization of terminal services**: Applications are run on servers within the internal network, with only **Keyboard/Mouse/Video (KVM)** information relayed over the standard SSL port between the user's computer and the internal network.

- **Establishment of a network connection over SSL**

Establishing Network Connectivity over SSL

Another mechanism of delivering remote access to non-web applications over an SSL connection is to establish a remote network connection over SSL, that is, to assign the remote machine an internal IP address, and treat it as a node on the internal network using an IPSEC-like model. Establishing network connections over SSL is sometimes considered as a feature in itself (and not just as a method of delivering access to non-web applications). As such we have given it its own section within this chapter.

To establish the connection, the SSL VPN sends some code (typically an ActiveX control or Java applet) to the user's machine and thereby creates a "virtual network adapter" on the user's machine. It then assigns the user an IP address on the internal network, and uses the SSL tunnel to establish a network connection between the internal network and the remote node. In many ways this method of communication parallels IPSec VPN technology, virtual network adapters can usually relay all network traffic—TCP, UDP, IP, ICMP, etc.

The entire network packet is encrypted using SSL and put within the payload of a new packet that is transmitted using regular TCP/IP networking as seen below:

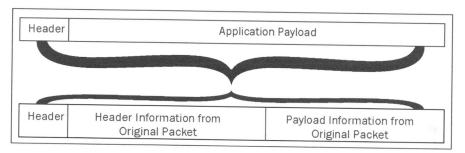

Two basic variants of network-type tunneling may be used:

- **Full tunneling**: All network traffic generated on the user's computer (TCP/IP, UDP/IP, ICMP, etc.) is sent to the SSL VPN server. The SSL VPN server routes traffic intended for internal systems to those machines, and sends traffic intended for the Internet out through the gateways used for all of the other Internet-bound traffic from the organization.

- **Split tunneling**: The user's computer sends all SSL VPN related traffic (i.e., traffic intended for internal systems) over the tunnel, but routes Internet-bound traffic (or any other non-SSL VPN related network communications) through its normal default gateway.

Furthermore, SSL VPN network-type tunnels may or may not be fully bi-directional:

- **Fully bi-directional**: the network connection that is established over SSL works in both directions, that is, from the user to the SSL VPN server (and its network) and from the SSL VPN server (and its network) back to the user. This is the type of SSL VPN tunnel that best mimics users' LAN connection as they normally have when in their office. A user could issue a *ping* to a machine on the internal network, and an administrator working on the internal network could issue a ping to the user's remote computer.

- **Partially bi-directional**: The tunnel does not function as a true bi-directional network connection as some types of communication cannot be initiated from the SSL VPN server's side of the connection. There are many possibilities for such limitations. One example would be a connection that allows TCP to flow freely in both directions but does not allow the initiation of ICMP communications from the SSL VPN server to the client. So a user can ping a server on the internal network (i.e., send ICMP ECHO packets and receive ICMP ECHO REPLY responses), but no machines on the internal network can ping the user's computer

Sometimes, SSL VPN products offer the ability to deliver access using more than one of the aforementioned technologies, in which case the methods offered are usually referred to as **modes of operation**. For example, an SSL VPN may offer Web application type access for Web simple applications (to be discussed in the next section), port forwarding for more complicated access, and network level access for system administrators. We will discuss when to use which mode when discussing security (in Chapter 4).

Why Different Access Technologies for Web Applications

It should be noted that some of the aforementioned methods of handling remote access to non-Web applications (network tunneling, port forwarding, and terminal services) could also be used to provide remote access to Web applications. However, using such techniques to provide access to Web-based applications curtails the benefits of SSL VPN. Web access is available from essentially any machine with a Web browser, while the non-Web handling technologies require stronger technology at the client (for example, the ability to run applets, greater OS permissions, etc.) and is available from more limited number of systems. Furthermore, performance is likely to be better when using the native web communications than when using terminal services to display the contents of a web browser run on a server back in the office. Also, as will be discussed in Chapter 4, it is not wise to establish network connectivity between machines not known to be secure and your corporate network, so, even if a machine the machines that can run applets to establish network tunneling over SSL

Applets

The need to tunnel non-web traffic over SSL (and the desire to establish network connections over SSL) introduced us to the concept of **applets**. In the context of SSL VPN technology, applets are relatively small pieces of code utilized by SSL VPNs to perform various tasks on computers used for remote access. Applets may manage the client side of a network connection tunneled over SSL, intercept requests to specific IP-Port combinations and relay them via the SSL tunnel, or interface with the operating system components.

As we explore SSL VPN technology, we will see that applets play a great role not only in delivering the functionality capabilities of SSL VPN technology, but also in performing numerous security-related tasks.

Remote Access to Files and Other Resources

In the context of SSL VPN technology, two types of file access that must be considered:

1. Remote mounting of network drives
2. File access interface

Remote Mounting of Network Drives

Remote Mounting of drives refers to the ability of an SSL VPN to allow remote users to access network drives (including home directories) as if the users were in their offices. Besides serving as a convenience, allowing remote drive mounting serves another purpose—some applications may have links to files or directories using common share names, and may not work unless remote mounting is possible. Example of mounting would be to allow users to access z:\ from Windows Explorer on the machine used to access the SSL VPN—where z:\ is a standard network share on the internal network as shown in the following figure (note the network-drive icon in the address bar):

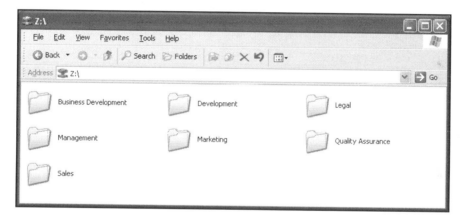

This capability is normally delivered over SSL using one of the methods we described earlier—by establishing network connectivity over SSL, relaying SMB-related traffic through the forwarding the appropriate ports, and so on.

> Remote mounting capabilities vary between SSL VPN products, as does support for specific file repositories (Novell Netware, Microsoft Windows, Unix NFS mounts, and so on).

File Access Interface

SSL VPNs typically offer some GUI-based interface for remote users to access files. Typically, people can upload, download, or search for files within a specific network share or their home directories. A file interface may mimic Windows Explorer, provide an FTP-like GUI, or look completely different from other system tools. A sample file access interface appears below (courtesy of Whale Communications):

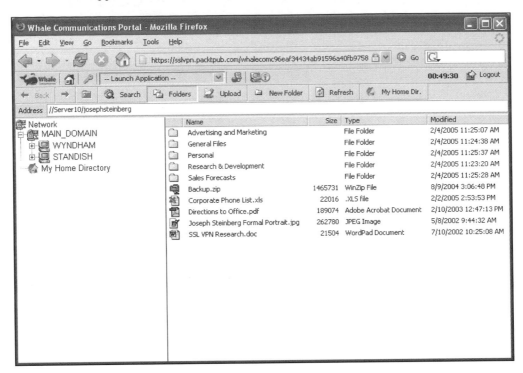

Telnet and Host Access

SSL VPNs can also provide users with the ability to Telnet to internal systems either through the use of the Telnet utility present on the access device (e.g., telnet.exe on MS Windows machines) or through the use of a special applet that is delivered by the SSL VPN. SSL VPNs typically also support mainframe access using Telnet-3270 or Telnet-5250 protocols. Such access may require that special mainframe-access software be present on the access device or may use a download of the necessary code from the SSL VPN server. Access is achieved either by establishing a network connection over SSL and relaying traffic as if the user were local, or by intercepting port requests, etc. as discussed earlier.

A demonstration of mainframe access via an SSL VPN is shown in the following figure (Screenshot courtesy of Netilla Networks):

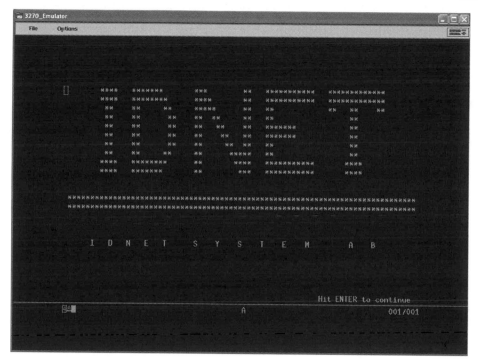

Printers and Other Network Resources

SSL VPN technology can allow remote users to print on printers in their offices from thousands of miles away or to send faxes through corporate fax servers even when not in the office. As was the case with file access, SSL VPNs utilize the technologies described above to deliver these types of capabilities.

Terminal Services

One area that deserves special attention is **Terminal Services**. Remote access to Terminal Services is offered by most SSL VPNs and is achieved in a similar fashion to other non-web applications. However, it is interesting to note that some Terminal-Services type products are often used as remote access solutions in themselves, especially for non-web applications. If an organization's critical systems are available internally via Terminal Services they'll work remotely if Terminal Services are opened to the Internet.

Of course, if Terminal Services will be Internet accessible, it is critical to ensure that the Terminal Services implementation remains secure. It is wise in such situations to consider deploying an SSL VPN, Application Firewall, or other security technology to manage remote access to the Terminal Services infrastructure. Also, as Terminal Services is an extremely inefficient way to provide remote access to web-enabled applications, thought should be given to deploying an SSL VPN as the remote access gateway and servicer of web-application requests, with Terminal Services handling non-web traffic.

Terminal Services (and related technologies) can also allow users to access their own desktops from anywhere—another reason to consider incorporating Terminal Services type technologies into a remote access strategy.

Internet-Enabling Internal Applications

One of the major enhancements to reverse proxy technology introduced by SSL VPNs is the ability to transform internal applications into systems that can be accessed across the Internet. We have already examined how non-Web applications can be extended for use across the Internet. Now we look at web-based applications.

Web-Based Applications

Web applications offer a web interface and are normally accessed using a web browser. At first glance, it may seem that providing SSL-based remote access to web applications should be a trivial task—just convert all of the internal HTTP traffic to SSL-encrypted HTTPS traffic—but this is not the case. Web applications designed for use on an intranet often include code sections that pose serious problems when planning a remote-access deployment. Several examples of this are:

- **The use of internal IP numbers**: There are several ranges of IP addresses reserved for internal IP addressing schemes, and which are not routable across the Internet (as defined in RFC 1918, available at `http://www.faqs.org/rfcs/rfc1918.html`). Addresses within some of these ranges, however, are often used in environments in which **Network Address Translation (NAT)** is used to convert externally accessible addresses to addresses used on a local LAN. Although NAT is a wonderful technology, the use of internal numbering schemes poses problems when one wants to provide SSL-based remote access. Any server references that use internal numbering schemes within web applications will not work remotely. NAT servers translate only addresses within the network portion of packet headers. They do not analyze and translate addresses within the HTML or XML code of a web page. So, a link to `http://192.168.1.2/page45.asp` will be converted by the SSL VPN (which overlays SSL encryption) to `https://192.168.1.2/page45.asp`. But, when such a link is clicked remotely, `192.168.1.2` will not be resolvable and the user will receive an error message.

Non-Routable IP Addresses include:

1. Class A - 10.0.0.0 through 10.255.255.255
2. Class B - 172.16.0.0 through 172.31.255.255
3. Class C - 192.168.0.0 through 192.168.255.255

- **The use of non-fully qualified machine names**: Machines that are local to a user in the office, and whose names can be resolved locally, will prove unreachable across the Internet if attempts are made to access them without fully qualified names. For example, a link such as `http://human-resources-server` may work when a user is in the office, but will not work across the Internet. Any references of such a construction in any Intranet applications or within e-mail messages will not work properly when users try to access them remotely.

- **The use of fully qualified machine names that are not DNS published or otherwise accessible from the Internet**: In addition to links containing names that are not fully qualified, other links may fail and Intranet applications may not work. For example, `server5.josephsteinberg.com` may be a valid server name on the author's LAN at home and references to it within an application will function properly when he uses the application via a wi-fi LAN connection from his living room. But, because this machine is not listed in any DNS server outside the author's house, attempts to remotely access such a machine using the aforementioned name will fail.

- **Links built within JavaScript, Java applets, ActiveX, Macromedia Flash code, etc.**: Such links may contain internal references as described above. Because they are built within code, such links may not appear to exist when reviewing the sources of pages served by applications and/or the SSL VPN server. Yet, if they are not translated, portions of application may not function properly.

So how does an SSL VPN enable remote access when applications have references that will not work across the Internet?

It translates internal references to an externally accessible format. The implementation of such translation differs between SSL VPN products. Some common approaches include:

- **Passing information about internal references as a parameter**: When translation is implemented using such a scheme, links containing internal references are converted to a URL of the following format:
  ```
  https://SSL-VPN-NAME/somepage.html?RealLocation
          =InternalInformation
  ```

  For security reasons, the internal information passed may be encrypted within the source of the pages accessed via the SSL VPN. For example:
  ```
  https://SSL-VPN-NAME/somepage.html?RealLocation
          =SomeEncryptedString
  ```

- **Modification of the URL to add information**: Instead of passing the information as a parameter, the information is added to the URL as if it were **directory structure information**. For example:
  ```
  https://SSL-VPN-NAME/InternalInformation/somepage.html
  ```

As described above, this may be encrypted and appear more like:
`https://SSL-VPN-NAME/EncryptedString/somepage.html`

- **Tunnel all as non-web**: One of the serious drawbacks of performing translation is that, as is the case with human-language translation engines, application-level translation engines are not perfect. Some references that require translation may not be translated or may be translated incorrectly. For example, websites may use compiled flash code that contains links, but many SSL VPNs cannot understand what references are built within complied code, and as a result, may be unable to translate such links. Java applets may build URLs in numerous manners and an SSL VPN may therefore miss some of the translations it needs to perform.

  One simple technique used by SSL VPNs to avoid the problems of missed translations is not to translate altogether and instead utilize network connectivity over SSL even for web-based applications. The remote user's computer becomes a node on the internal network and can access any application—web or non-web. As mentioned previously, this approach effectively emulates IPSec-type connectivity, but uses an SSL tunnel instead of an IPSec tunnel. This offers the advantage of ensuring that applications will be available remotely without the fear of missed translations or mistranslations. At the same time, as mentioned earlier network, tunneling severely limits the number of machines from which access can be securely provided. This creates new security concerns, which will be discussed in Chapter 4.

- **Handle complex web applications**: As was mentioned earlier, terminal services type access can be used to handle complex web applications, but doing so often curtails the number of devices from which access is possible and also hurts performance.

Commonly, SSL VPNs offer translation and utilize lower-level tunneling as a backup for applications for which the tunneling does not work.

Many of today's most powerful web-based applications do not rely on simple HTML to deliver their user interfaces; often Java or ActiveX controls are utilized. These types of technologies extend the functionality of the web browser both in terms of user interface and in terms of communication.

Although some Java and ActiveX applets pose no difficulties for SSL VPNs, others can be quite a challenge. Often these types of technologies are the culprits for requiring the use of lower-level tunneling in lieu of just web-type translation.

Remote Access Interface

The third major enhancement to reverse-proxy technology offered by SSL VPNs is the ability to provide a suitable experience for remote users. Several important components of the user experience provided by SSL VPNs are described in detail below:

Login and Single Sign On

As the gateway into a user's business environment, SSL VPNs obviously demand proper authentication before allowing access. As such, they do not allow users to establish sessions and send requests to internal servers until users have proven their identities.

Although a username and password combination is clearly the most common form of online authentication, SSL VPNs typically support other methods of authentication as well. Third-party authentication engines providing RADIUS or LDAP interfaces are commonly leveraged in SSL VPN implementations. Other authentication methods include one-time password systems, tokens, smart cards, USB authentication devices, client certificates, biometrics, and **Public Key Infrastructure (PKI)**-based authentication. These authentication techniques are usually better at assuring users' identities than username-password combinations (as will be discussed in Chapter 4). However, it is important to realize, that if specialized devices are required for authentication (for example, a USB token or fingerprint reader), users may be unable to achieve remote access from some public or borrowed computers.

Regardless of the method of authentication, it is important to offer users the convenience of logging in once, rather than having to submit credentials each time they access an internal system. Various SSL VPN products offer different methods of achieving **Single Sign On (SSO)**—they typically fall into one of these three flavors:

- Upon the user's initial login, passwords are collected from the user for each system to be accessed. These credentials are stored in a database on the SSL VPN appliance, and, upon subsequent logins to the SSL VPN, the SSL VPN can automatically log the user into any system for which it has a stored password. This paradigm of offering SSO offers the advantage of simple set up, but among its drawbacks are the need to protect the database of credentials and the issues associated with managing duplicate repositories of authentication information (the need to keep the two stores synchronized, to delete users from multiple databases if they leave the company, etc.)

- The SSL VPN is integrated with third-party authentication and authorization databases. Credentials for access to internal systems are maintained in the third-party systems, either stored there during a user's initial SSL VPN session as described above, or entered into the database prior to use of the SSL VPN if the SSO system is used internally as well. Upon attempts to access applications, the SSL VPN extracts the credentials from the external database and automatically logs the user on.

- The SSL VPN does not maintain any credential information, but rather collects all necessary information on the login page when users log in. This method simplifies credential management and avoids the aforementioned security concerns, but may require users to enter multiple passwords each time they authenticate.

A combination of these techniques may also be used. For example, an SSL VPN may store and extract passwords for general internal systems from a database, but require the user to enter authentication information for more sensitive systems each time he or she logs in. Similarly, an SSL VPN may implement SSO for most systems—but require a login (after a user has already logged into the SSL VPN) if the user wants to access an especially sensitive system.

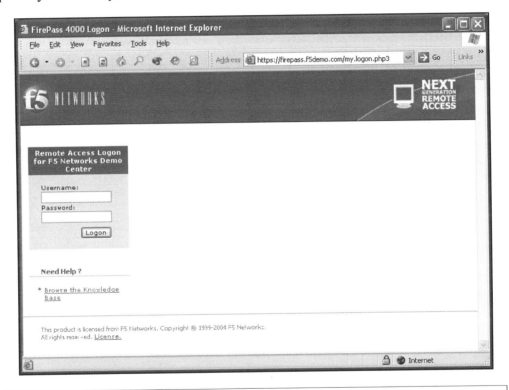

SSL VPNs typically allow login pages to be customized so that they appear uniform with other corporate web pages. Elements such as corporate logos, warnings against unauthorized access, and the like are often incorporated into the login page. Of course, if SSO requires collecting multiple credentials on the login page, the page will need to be customized accordingly.

Portal Pages

After users successfully log in to an SSL VPN, they are typically presented with some form of **portal page**, sometimes known as a **home page** or **menu page**, from where they can choose which applications they wish to access.

Portal pages and the elements present on such pages vary between SSL VPN products. Some items that are typically found on portal pages include:

- **Name and logo of the company**: This is usually customizable when the SSL VPN is configured.

- **Application Menus**: A list of applications from which users may choose applications that they wish to access.

- **Bookmarks**: Personal bookmarks for each individual user to applications, files, folders, or other resources. The system administrator may set up standard bookmarks on an individual, group, or enterprise-wide basis. Sometimes users may set up their own personal bookmarks as well.

- **Helper applications**: These may be links to any useful utilities such as:
  - A link to download useful tools. For example a link to download a Microsoft Word document viewer might be useful for users who will be accessing Word documents remotely but may not have Word installed on every machine from which they will be using the SSL VPN.
  - A link to display a basic calendar
  - A link to display a calculator

- **News**: Corporate news bulletins or announcements

- **File Access**: Access to either a user-friendly interface from which files can be accessed, the ability to trigger remote mounting of network drives and/or home directories, or both

- **Internal URL entry space**: A space where users can enter URLs that are normally valid only on the internal network (for example those that refer to machines not publicly DNS listed) and browse as if they were sitting in their office using the LAN

- **Clock or Timer**: Displays the duration of the current SSL VPN session, time until the next forced re-authentication, time elapsed since the last user activity, or time remaining until the next inactivity timeout (unless the user performs some action)

- **Toolbars**: A bar of icons for fast access to various SSL VPN functions. Toolbars are described in more detail below.

- **Help**: Access to online help

Portal pages are typically customizable; of course, the level of flexibility varies between SSL VPN products. Some customization capabilities are made available to individual users, some are typically left under the control of administrators. Some SSL VPN products offer scripting capabilities that allow administrators to not only customize the portal page, but also to extend its functionality.

Vis-à-vis customization: Two areas in which many SSL VPNs allow significant customization are home pages and bookmark lists. Home page layouts and contents typically configured by administrators can be configured on a per-user, per-user-group, or per-organization basis. This offers enterprises the flexibility to provide specific users with menu choices of only those applications that are appropriate for those individuals. For example, an engineer working in the MIS department may see Telnet and a Trouble-Ticket Tracking System, whereas an accountant in the finance department may see the Accounts Receivable and Accounts Payable systems. Bookmarks typically vary from user to user.

> Some enterprises have existing portal implementations and, if their SSL VPN server supports such a capability, they might choose to utilize their standard portal page as the portal page displayed when users access the SSL VPN.

Toolbars

Toolbars, which typically appear on either the top or left of SSL VPN windows within a web browser (although they could be located elsewhere), provide users with a mechanism to quickly and easily navigate between applications. Toolbars may also have other components such as access to online help, access to helper applications, and other items discussed earlier in reference to the portal page. Toolbars may be customizable by either individual users or the SSL VPN administrator.

Languages

There are several considerations when it comes to languages:

- **Support for applications using non-Latin character sets**: Multi-national corporations or entities conducting business with overseas partners often have applications or data that include non-Latin characters and these characters will need to be rendered by the SSL VPN.

- **Multi-Lingual User Interface**: To ensure maximum productivity, users need an interface in the language that they normally use for conducting business in their respective locales. Language selection may be performed by automatically setting the language based on the browser's language settings, may be manually configured by the user, or may be set by administrators on a user/group basis. Portal pages, error messages, toolbars, etc. would all appear in the language with which the user is comfortable.

- **Foreign version compatibility**: The ability of any of the SSL VPN's downloadable code (i.e., applets) to run on systems running foreign versions of their operating system. Also, the ability of its administrative tools to run on such operating systems

- **Multi-Lingual Administrative Tools Interface**: The ability of the Administrative Tools to offer interfaces in languages other than English.

Multiple Windows Vs. a Single Window

Some SSL VPNs allow multiple applications to be opened in one window and provide the user with a toolbar or some other method of navigating between them. Others spawn individual windows for each application instance in use. Each method has its advantages and disadvantages; ideally, which method is used should be up to the user, but, as of today, the product vendor or the SSL VPN system administrator typically determines it.

Logout Button

A Logout button affords users the ability to log out of the SSL VPN using a single click. After a user clicks Logout, the SSL VPN session is terminated and access to all internal applications is severed until the user logs in again.

Help

Online help, which may be accessible from an SSL VPN toolbar, from the portal page, or both, is exactly what it sounds like. Help includes answering the typical questions that most users have when using an SSLVPN, and provides contact information for the helpdesk servicing SSL VPN and remote access users.

User Interface Based on Browser Type

With the proliferation of Internet-enabled **Personal Data Assistants (PDA)** and other handheld devices, the ability to access important systems and information from anywhere has grown dramatically. The sophistication of today's handheld computers and the processing power now available in portable form factors enables SSL VPN technology to provide access from devices that literally fit in pockets. In fact, many SSL VPN products now offer technology to accommodate access from systems running operating environments such as WindowsCE/Pocket PC, PalmOS, and Symbian OS.

One important technical feature offered by SSL VPNs technology is the ability to adjust the SSL VPN GUI based on the type of device used for access. It is obvious that on a small device a web browser cannot possibly display a full-sized browser screen in a readable format; a miniature interface is necessary. Also, wireless bandwidth constraints can render intolerable the time it takes to load graphically rich pages or other multimedia that may be used without issue over the wired Internet; fewer images and sounds are common in handheld-optimized web pages.

Today's SSL VPNs do not typically offer the same degree of access from handheld devices as they do from regular computers. Although most SSL VPNs do support access to web-based applications from small devices, due to the limitations of the devices they often do not support network-level connectivity or other forms of access to non-web applications. Mounting of remote drives is also not usually available, although a file access GUI may be. Some of these shortcomings stem from the inability of handheld devices to run the ActiveX or Java controls necessary to implement full remote access. Nonetheless, as many key applications now offer web interfaces, the ability to access web-based applications from handheld devices can prove quite valuable to an organization. Also, as vendors produce new generations of handheld devices, these shortcomings may disappear.

SSL VPN Status Window

As part of the software that SSL VPNs use to handle tunneling of non-web communications over SSL, there may be a status window that can be viewed on the client machine. This window may indicate the internal IP number assigned to the user's machine (if a network connection is established over SSL), the external IP address of the machine, which ports are being monitored and having their contents transferred to the internal network, the number of bytes transferred, and other pertinent information about the client machine and SSL VPN session.

Most users will not need to refer to this window under normal circumstances; the information in it may be helpful to helpdesk and support personnel if there are communication difficulties that they are trying to diagnose and correct.

Web Email (WebMail) Interfaces

Some SSL VPNs come equipped with basic web-based e-mail (WebMail) interfaces that allow users to read and send e-mail without having to use a fully functional e-mail client or even a standard WebMail system such as Microsoft Outlook Web Access or Lotus iNotes. The WebMail interfaces offered by SSL VPNs are usually quite rudimentary and likely to work from a large number of devices. This enables basic access to e-mail even from handhelds and other low-end browsers from which access via standard e-mail application software may not be possible. At the same time it introduces a new interface to the user, which may lead to user confusion.

Administration Tools

Every SSL VPN product offers its own unique administration tools—some are web based and some use proprietary clients and some offer varying degrees of integration with general network and computer management systems via **SNMP (Simple Network**

Management Protocol). Some also integrate with SYSLOG to simplify analysis of their audit logs.

As described earlier, SSL VPNs are typically regular computers running software. As such, some degree of operating system management for the device may be necessary—so administration will likely entail interaction with Linux or Windows. From time to time, for example, administrators may need to apply Operating System patches to ensure that the SSL VPN remains secure and properly hardened against attack.

Performance

To boost performance SSL VPNs utilize various techniques including:

- SSL Acceleration
- Compression of HTTP traffic
- Caching
- Load Balancing

SSL Acceleration

Running complex cryptographic algorithms (including asymmetric algorithms) on a computer utilizes significant amounts of CPU cycles. As such, SSL processing presents potential issues of hindering system performance. An SSL VPN server could expend significant resources on its SSL overhead even before catering to any of the remote access business functions. SSL processing alone can significantly reduce the number of user requests a server (including an SSL VPN) can process simultaneously.

SSL Accelerators offload SSL processing from computers' main CPU, freeing the processor to handle more user requests. SSL Accelerators come in two form factors—as cards that can be inserted into a server and as external devices that are situated on the same network as servers for which they handle SSL processing. While SSL VPNs support both forms, some SSL VPN products offer accelerator technology as a standard function, some as an optional add on, and others offer support for external accelerator devices. In any fashion in which it is used, acceleration may significantly boost performance of an SSL VPN.

Compression of HTTP Traffic

The code (HTML, XML, JavaScript, ASP, and so on) used in web pages such as those served by the SSL VPN for its own user interface as well as for the web applications behind it consists of ASCII text—a data format that is highly compressible using standard compression techniques. Because many users may access the SSL VPN over slow Internet connections, compressing the HTML can yield a major improvement in their remote-access experience.

For several years, web browsers and servers have offered such compression as part of their content-encoding and transfer-encoding feature set as provided for in the HTTP 1.1 standard. As part of the initiation of a web session, a capable browser signals the web server with which it is communicating that it is capable of supporting compression and which method of compression it prefers (usually gzip). If the web server also supports such compression, the server will begin sending compressed web traffic to the browser. This may be done by sending pre-compressed versions of static web pages or by dynamically compressing pages as they are being sent. When the browser receives such data, it decompresses it and then renders the contents of the data as it would normally. The additional processing load on the server to compress the data, and on the browser to decompress it, usually pales in comparison with the time saved by transmitting less data across the Internet (especially if the pages sent are pre-compressed). Of course, if a browser does not support compression it will not signal the server and compression will not be used.

Caching

SSL VPN servers may cache certain pages or page elements that are likely to be requested multiple times during a user's session. By doing so, they may reduce the amount of internal communications that need to take place in order to reply to user requests and thereby improve performance.

Load Balancing: IP Spraying

Another method used to boost performance of SSL VPNs is to utilize multiple SSL VPN appliances concurrently. The technique of dividing the remote-access load among multiple systems is known as **load balancing** and is used not only to improve performance, but also to ensure that the failure of a single SSL VPN server does not lead to a total remote-access outage.

In a common form of load balancing in SSL VPN environments, all of the SSL VPN appliances appear to users as a single server with a single name and IP address. When users send requests to this SSL VPN the load balancer hardware/software divides the HTTP requests among the real SSL VPN servers. Such a load-balancing scheme is known as **IP Spraying**.

Most SSL VPNs offer load balancing as an option. Some offer the necessary technology within their appliances so that the SSL VPN appliances themselves manage the load balancing and route requests accordingly as seen in the following diagram.

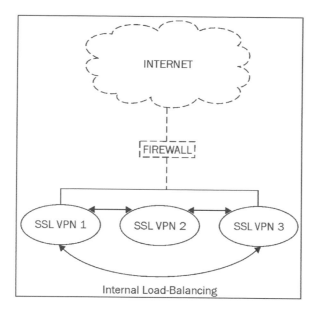

Internal Load-Balancing

Even those SSL VPN products that lack an innate load-balancing capability can often be used in a load-balancing configuration through the addition of an external third-party load-balancing device placed in front of multiple SSL VPN appliances as shown below:

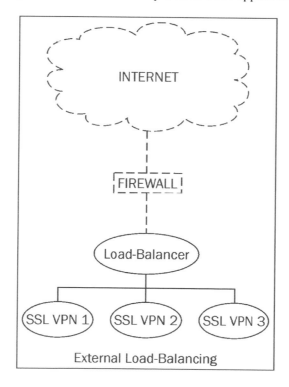

External Load-Balancing

Access from Older Web Browsers

We discussed earlier the need to accommodate handheld devices and the inferior conditions present on such equipment. The challenge of providing access from substandard browsers, however, did not begin with handheld devices.

The proliferation of Web browsers in the late 1990s coupled with general adversity to upgrading systems that are working without major problems has led to a large number of older browsers remaining in use around the world. Some of these browsers may not support or support only partially the technical requirements of popular SSL VPNs, and remote access may be limited or unavailable from them. Besides the issues of running ActiveX and Java controls as described when discussing handheld devices, older web browsers may be unable to support some GUI elements, or even acceptable SSL encryption levels.

Access from older browsers may also affect performance of the SSL VPN session. For example, many older browsers do not support compression of the HTTP data stream, a deficiency that can substantially reduce performance over slower modem connections.

The often-heard claim that SSL VPN technology allows access from *any* web browser has some truth in it, but exaggerates the real-world benefits of deploying the technology.

SSL VPN Sample Session

Now that we have covered how the components of SSL VPN technology work, let us examine how they work together during a sample user session:

1. The user enters the URL of the SSL VPN remote access system in the browser. In this example, we will use http://remote.packtpub.com.

2. If the user made the request on an unencrypted port (e.g., in our example we made an HTTP call to web port 80) the SSL VPN will redirect it to port 443 and begin using SSL encryption for all communication with the user. The redirection would be to https://remote.packtpub.com/. The SSL VPN will send the user a login page. (In truth, the SSL VPN may run various security checks on the system before sending the login page. We will discuss these checks in detail in Chapter 4.)

3. The user then submits his or her credentials (usually a username and password) to the SSL VPN.

4. If the credentials are acceptable, the SSL VPN presents the user with a portal page and downloads the necessary ActiveX or Java code to tunnel non-web traffic over SSL or to establish a network type connection over SSL.

5. The user selects a Web-based application to use from the portal and the SSL VPN logs the user into that system. The SSL VPN translates all communications from the internal system before relaying them to the user.

6. When the user clicks on a link within the application, the SSL VPN translates the link from the external format it created back to the original internal format and relays the request to the appropriate server.

7. When any non-web traffic is required at the client, the SSL VPN agent on the user's machine encapsulates the data using one of the techniques described earlier and sends it over the SSL connection to the SSL VPN, which unbundles the traffic and restores it to its native format, and sends it on the internal network.

Summary

SSL VPNs utilize advanced technology to deliver remote access from web browsers. They are equipped to allow both web and non-web communications, and use sophisticated technologies to address the challenges presented by both types of traffic. They can even deliver a remote network connection.

The access granted by SSL VPN technology, however, pose serious security concerns, which is what we will now address in Chapter 4.

4
SSL VPN Security

SSL VPNs serve as gateways into corporate infrastructure and as such, security is a critical component of any SSL VPN offering. So important are the security-related capabilities of SSL VPN products that the differences in the security features set across products often determine which SSL VPN an enterprise will choose to deploy.

SSL VPN security falls into three categories:

- **Authentication and Authorization**: Users gain access to valuable information and systems through the SSL VPN. Because of this, it is critical to ensure that only authorized users access resources through the SSL VPN and that individual users access only those resources that they are supposed to access.

- **Endpoint Security**: Endpoint security is sometimes known as **Client-Side Security** or **Browser-Side Security**. It refers to technology implemented to prevent any security-related problems occurring on devices used to access resources via the SSL VPN. It is important to realize that as opposed to earlier remote-access technologies, SSL VPN technology allows access from machines not known to be secure and as such, the endpoint concerns are different from the endpoint issues present in older remote-access scenarios.

- **Server-Side Security**: Server-Side security, sometimes known as **Network Security**, refers to protecting internal corporate resources including the SSL VPN server itself from falling victim to any form of compromise.

Throughout our detailed review of these areas, it is important to keep in mind that SSL VPN products differ widely on how security is implemented. Each product does not necessarily offer all the features discussed, and due to product design and capability differences, some of the security issues may not even be pertinent when certain products are deployed. One should also be aware that some of the security functions described below are often implemented through the integration of third-party products with the core SSL VPN offering—sometimes by the SSL VPN vendor and sometimes by the implementer. In any case, the remainder of this chapter describes the security concerns associated with SSL VPN technology and some approaches to addressing them.

Authentication and Authorization

As discussed in Chapter 3, SSL VPNs typically require that users identify themselves and prove their identities before granting access to internal resources.

Authentication

Authentication is usually achieved using one or more of the following factors:

- Something only the user knows
- Something only the user has
- Something only the user is (i.e., a physical property of the user's person)

SSL VPN products support a variety of authentication schemes and leverage all three of the aforementioned methods of proving one's identity. Most commonly, users identify themselves using a username and authenticate using one of these several techniques:

Passwords

The user is supplied a secret password known only to the user and which is associated with the user's identification information (username). The SSL VPN compares this password to a copy of the password stored in a database or preferably performs a hash on the password and compares it to a previously hashed value of the correct password stored in a database. If the comparison results in a perfect match, it grants the user access with the permissions appropriate for that specific user.

One-Time Passwords

Users are provided with some mechanism of producing passwords that can be used only once. After a user submits his or her username along with a correct one-time password, he or she is granted access. However, the particular password that was used for access will not be valid for subsequent login attempts. One-time passwords are often utilized through one of three systems:

- **A pre-arranged list of one-time passwords**: A list of one-time passwords is generated by the authentication system and given to the user while he or she is in office. Every time the user wishes to login remotely, he or she uses the next password from the list and crosses it out. When the list is exhausted (or almost exhausted), a new list is generated and provided to the user.

- **Hardware tokens or software that generates one-time passwords**: Products such as Vasco DigiPass or RSA SecurID made this concept popular. A small hardware device or a piece of software running on a handheld or laptop computer is used to generate a one-time password by combining the system's timestamp, a unique key, and other information. The

70

authentication server has information about the token's unique key and can generate the same one-time password for any time at which the user attempts to login. The value the user submits is compared with the value generated by the authentication system and if they match, the user is given access.

- **Challenge-Response Based Tokens or Software**: The authentication server presents the user with some number (or string of characters) that the user enters into his or her hardware token or software system. The token or software utility generates a code based on the input. That code is sent to the authentication server. The authentication server compares the user's input with the expected response that it generates based on the original code and if they match, the user is given access.

Biometric Information

Biometrics, which refers to verifying physical attributes of humans in order to guarantee the identity of a user, is not used often for SSL VPN access. Biometric readers are not ubiquitous, and as such, requiring biometric-type authentication would severely decrease the number of points from which users could access resources via an SSL VPN. However, biometrics can be used to authenticate users for privileged sessions—the implementation of a scheme in which users logging in with a username and password are given access, but users who login using biometric-based authentication are provided with access to more resources. This concept will be discussed in detail in the *Tiers of Access Based on Endpoint Situation* section later in this chapter.

Client Certificates

Digital certificates (which are an example of "something the user has") can be used to authenticate users to SSL VPNs. However, it should be noted that their use is often limited to machines upon which the certificates can safely be installed. Clearly, it is not feasible to use such an authentication scheme for access from Internet kiosks, which usually do not offer the user access to floppy/CD drives, or to USB ports. Furthermore, if client certificates represent something that a user has and that other people do not have, it would be extremely unwise to load a certificate onto a borrowed or public computer where it could potentially be obtained by other parties. As such, client certificates are often used only for authentication from specific secure devices.

Smart Cards or USB Tokens

Small physical devices designed specifically for use with authentication systems are commercially available. Alternatively, client certificates or encrypted passwords may be stored on such devices.

Two-Factor Authentication

SSL VPN products also allow usage of two-factor authentication. **Two-factor authentication** refers to authentication that requires the user to authenticate using two different methods of authentication, for example, providing a password that only he or she knows and a code number from a hardware token that only he or she has. Two-factor authentication is usually stronger than single-factor authentication; however, a single strong method of authentication will likely be more effective than two different poorly implemented systems.

One noteworthy point: Sometimes people suggest that users can be identified based on the IP address of the device that they are using for access. It is important to realize that in the case of SSL VPN technology, this poses some serious problems. The SSL VPN value proposition, as discussed in Chapter 2, relies on the fact that remote access can be achieved from diverse machines. Hence administrators do not wish to limit the computers from which users may achieve access via the SSL VPN. Therefore, we cannot rely on the IP number of the user's computer (or any other related information) for any clue as to the user's identity. Users may use the SSL VPN from a new computer on a regular basis. They may also use public computers or borrow each other's computers for remote-access use. Furthermore, the proliferation of **NAT (Network Address Translation)** means that many users using different computers on the same LAN may appear to the SSL VPN server as if they are using the same machine IP wise, and the widespread use of DHCP and other dynamic IP assignment mechanisms means that users IP addresses may change between SSL VPN sessions.

Despite these problems with IP-based authentication, IP addresses may be used in conjunction with other computer-based information to identify machines as trusted (as discussed later in this chapter when we discuss *Tiers of Access* and *Trusted Endpoints*). At the same time it should be clear that IP addresses should not be used to authenticate *users* of an SSL VPN.

Single Sign On

As was described in Chapter 3, SSL VPNs typically offer some form of **Single Sign On (SSO)** capability—that is, they do not require users to authenticate to each application being accessed during every session. Rather, they utilize some mechanism for collecting credentials that minimizes the number of times users need to authenticate. For more information on Single Sign On as it pertains to SSL VPN technology, please refer to the *Login and Single Sign On* section in Chapter 3.

Authorization

In the context of SSL VPN technology, **authorization** refers to granting an authenticated user rights to access specific applications and/or to read, modify, add, or delete specific files or data. Authorization takes place through several different avenues.

Operating System Permissions

Access to some applications or files may be controlled by operating system permissions (e.g., **Access Control Lists** or **ACLs**) that define which users may access specific resources. Operating system controls work in a similar fashion for remote users and for users working in their offices. When users attempt to access resources, the operating system determines if they have rights to access the resource in the fashion in which they are attempting to do so and allows or denies access accordingly.

File System Permissions

Computers whose file systems are being accessed may govern access rights to directories and files through standard ACLs or other file system controls that define access rights for particular users and user groups regardless of the users' locations. This is often implemented as part of an operating system, but may be done though an add-on package.

Native Application Permissions

Some applications require authentication before granting access. Based on user identity, specific functions within such an application (or the entire application) may be made available or blocked, and specific user activities within the application may be allowed or prohibited. Controls of this nature would work in a similar fashion for remote users and for users working in their offices.

Restricted Interfaces

An SSL VPN can also block a user from accessing specific resources by restricting the user's interface to one that does not include a link to such resources. A restricted interface may be utilized via the SSL VPN to prevent a user from seeing a utility that he or she is not authorized to use. (Smart security policy dictates that if a user is not supposed to access a system or file, it is wise not to advertise to them the fact that the system or file is availability to other parties.) Implementing a restricted interface reduces helpdesk calls—users do not call and ask why they see that a specific application is available but cannot access it.

Authorization Information Maintained by the SSL VPN

When users access remotely, the access permissions they receive may be different from what they would normally have when they access from inside their offices. This is especially true if a **Tiers-of-Access** system (as described later in this chapter) is implemented. When authorization information differs for remote sessions, data related to who can access what remotely is often stored in databases local to the SSL VPN server. Users who are not allowed to access specific resources via the SSL VPN (even if they can access the same resources when they are in their offices) will not be given access to such resources by the SSL VPN.

Third-Party Authorization Databases

Another place where authorization information for local and remote users can be stored is in third-party authorization databases. Commercial off-the-shelf authorization products have been around for several years and many SSL VPNs integrate with such systems.

End Point Security Concerns

Endpoint security concerns include:

- Sensitive data remaining in insecure locations
- Users neglecting to log out
- Viruses reaching internal networks the SSL VPN
- Worms reaching internal networks via tunnels created by the SSL VPN
- Hackers accessing the corporate network by bridging networks via the SSL VPN

The Problem: Sensitive Data in Insecure Locations

During the course of a remote access session, users may download proprietary, sensitive, or confidential information to the devices that they use for access. Although private data was certainly stored on access devices during the era of earlier remote-access technologies, such data maintenance was not a problem as users gained access only from corporate devices assigned to them. Such devices were intended to store sensitive information. However, with the advent of SSL VPN and the expectation that users will access corporate resources from public or borrowed computers, storage of data on devices used for access poses a serious risk.

Some of the information stored on an access device may be intentionally stored on the computer on a temporary basis. For example, a user who utilizes an SSL VPN's file-access capabilities and downloads a spreadsheet to examine may save the file to the local disk. If this file contains private information, for example sales projections for the upcoming year, it is essential that the spreadsheet be removed from the access device when the user completes the session.

What is perhaps more threatening to the confidentiality of sensitive information than the files that users know about are the large amounts of data that are stored on access devices without users' knowledge.

Browser Cache Entries

To improve performance, web browsers usually store local copies of web pages, images, and multimedia files that the users access. Doing so enables the browser to load such elements much faster in the event that the user returns to the same web page (or even to a different web page that uses some of the same elements, as is quite common). However, what improves performance for general web users also creates a serious security concern for SSL VPN users; SSL VPN users do not want other people who subsequently use the machine used for accessing the SSL VPN to be able to load any information accessed during the SSL VPN session.

Proprietary Cache Entries

Some applications (including some well-known commercial-off-the-shelf packages) do not use standard system caches for storing their temporary data. Instead, they utilize their own proprietary cache systems and store data in non-standard locations within local file systems. Data written to such caches should be removed upon completion of an SSL VPN session. Also, as will be discussed in detail later in this chapter, third-party search tools running on machines used to access an SSL VPN may also create cached versions of files accessed during an SSL VPN session in their own proprietary caches.

Temporary Files: Viewing E-mail Attachments

Similarly, temporary files are created on the access device when users access e-mail attachments via a Webmail interface through an SSL VPN. In many cases, such files are not automatically removed by the e-mail systems when users complete their sessions—so subsequent users might be able to view the contents of any e-mail attachment that a user opens remotely. Encrypting email attachments—which would make the attachments unreadable to unauthorized parties—usually does not solve this problem for two reasons:

- The files are usually cached when they are being accessed in their native applications—such as a document in Microsoft Word. This happens *after* they are decrypted.

- Decryption capabilities may not be available in the Webmail interface rendering access impossible from many locations.

Password protecting all email attachments (for example, using the password protection capabilities available in Word, Excel, etc.) is also not a solution as:

- Not all applications offer password protection for data
- Password mechanisms in many applications are weak; passwords can easily be circumvented or cracked
- Requiring passwords for all email attachments is impractical—users will not acquiesce to such an inconvenience.

We need a better solution to the problem of cached email attachments.

Temporary Files: Downloading and other Mechanisms

This problem is identical to the problem of e-mail attachments—just with a different mechanism of originally delivering the information to the access device.

Form-Field Contents Memorized for AutoComplete

When users are presented with forms to complete online, they often notice that the values for common fields are suggested to them after they begin typing their data into form fields. This is because web browsers typically cache user input to common text-entry fields to expedite completion of future forms. A user who enters an e-mail address on one web page that asks for such information is likely to need to enter the same input when prompted for identical information by another website. To reduce the amount of manual work, the computer offers the user the ability to reuse his or her prior input. However, as was the case with caching of web elements, this feature (often know as AutoComplete as it is called in the Microsoft Internet Explorer environment) poses a security risk to SSL VPN users. There may be data that users enter into forms during an SSL VPN session such as Social Security Numbers or the like that they do not want cached on access devices. If such information were cached, subsequent users could easily retrieve it, and such information could be abused for mischievous purposes such as identity theft.

URL Entries Memorized for AutoComplete

Similar to the form-field contents that are memorized, URLs accessed by users are stored in a cache on access devices. This allows users to type the beginning of a URL and have the computer suggest the rest of the URL making web browsing easier. As was the case with form fields, it is possible that private information will be contained within a URL (especially as a parameter to a system that was not designed with security in mind). There is also an issue of privacy—many people do not want others to know exactly which online resources they have used. So URLs accessed during a remote access session should not be left on public or borrowed computers for subsequent users to see.

Cookies Generated During User Sessions

Cookies are small text files placed onto access devices during web sessions that allow specific information to be remembered about the user for either the duration of the session, or for subsequent sessions. Cookies often store username information (and sometimes username and password combinations) for sites that users want to be able to access without having to enter their complete log in information each time they visit. Cookies are also often used to store personal preferences or settings for particular websites. As such, cookies can contain sensitive information, and while they provide tremendous value in terms of enhancing functionality and user experience, they should not be left on public/borrowed machines after an SSL VPN session is completed.

History Records

Browsers typically retain a history of web pages visited so that users who want to revisit a page but do not remember its URL can easily find what they want. But, history information can also reveal information about what a user did during a previous session and it might contain URLs that may disclose sensitive information (please see above). As such, history records pose a threat to SSL VPN users if left on machines not under organizational control.

User Credentials Memorized by the Browser

Some Web browsers offer users the option of storing username and password combinations so that they do not need to log in manually to pages demanding authentication. Obviously, SSL VPN users on borrowed or public machines should not elect to store such information on the device that they are using for access. However, if a user erred and instructed the browser to remember his or her credentials, the result would be a serious security risk. Furthermore, some credentials are cached even without prompting the user! For example, systems that utilize the HTTP Basic Authentication scheme cache the user's password during his or her session (to prevent having to prompt the user to re-enter a UID and password combination upon every request made to the server). Such a scheme will retain the password in a cache until the browser is either completely shut down or another user logs in and loads a new password into the cache.

Clearly, a significant amount of sensitive information may be left abandoned on insecure devices after users complete their SSL VPN sessions.

The Solution

There are several approaches taken by various SSL VPN products to address the problem of sensitive data being stored on access devices. Most commonly seen are the following:

- **Do nothing**: This approach is unacceptable for most organizations, but some lower-end SSL VPNs simply do not address the issue of data remaining on endpoint devices.

- **Warn the user**: Some low-end SSL VPNs do nothing on their own to prevent sensitive data from remaining, but warn the user upon logoff that he or she should eliminate any residue that may remain from the SSL VPN session. This approach is problematic as:

o   Removing cached information is not a simple task—as described above, there are numerous areas in which sensitive information may be stored. A user would need to be quite technically savvy in order to properly erase such information.

o   Even technically knowledgeable users may not have access to a tool that would perform a proper wipe of the disk space used to hold the sensitive information. An operating system DELETE or rm command (or their Windows equivalent) may not satisfactorily protect the sensitive information from being inappropriately accessed (this will be discussed later in this chapter).

o   What if the user never logged off—the browser crashes—so no warning is ever displayed?

- **Utilize NOCACHE commands**: Most of today's web browsers understand the command NOCACHE as sent by a web server to be an instruction not to cache data being accessed. Theoretically then, if the SSL VPN server embeds NOCACHE commands onto every page of data it sends to a user's computer, the problem of sensitive data being cached would be solved. Right?
  No. NOCACHE does *not* solve the problem for several reasons:

o   Not all browsers obey NOCACHE instructions.

o   Some applications may require local caching in order to function properly.

o   Turing off caching can severely affect performance and may render some applications essentially unusable, especially over a slow modem line.

o   NOCACHE does not prevent caching in AutoComplete stores, in history records, and other areas. It only instructs the browser not to cache the web elements that it receives. Temporary files will still be created by opening e-mail attachments and the resulting vulnerability will remain a security risk.

Despite these serious drawbacks, some lower-end SSL VPNs rely on NOCACHE instructions to implement security. Such solutions may be appropriate for specific projects and particular environments, but for general usage, one of the remaining two approaches for addressing cached data should be followed.

- **Wiping all cached data after a user session**: When a user completes a session, the SSL VPN erases all of the pertinent temporary information created during the session (as described above). No footprints are left behind. It is important to realize that the temporary information must be removed from the access device not only when a user logs out, but if a session is terminated for any other reason as well. Sessions may end when any of the following occurs:

o The user logs off

o Some pre-defined period of inactivity transpires

o Some pre-defined period of time elapses and a scheduled re-authentication event occurs, but the user does not properly re-authenticate within some specific period of time

o The browser crashes

o The browser is closed down

o The access device operating system crashes

o The system is shut down or rebooted

o Power is lost to the access device

When any of these events occurs, the SSL VPN should wipe the pertinent information from the access device. Obviously, in the case of a system crash or loss of power, the actual erasure may take place after a reboot.

- **Using encrypted virtual storage space that is removed after a session is completed**: The SSL VPN creates a designated section of memory and hard disk that it uses (and forces other utilities on the user's access device to use) to store all temporary information for the user's session. The entire contents of the memory section and disk are encrypted. The virtual storage space can be removed at the end of a session, but even if for some reason it were not, the information within it would be difficult, if not impossible, for unauthorized parties to access. While this solution may seem to be the simplest answer to the problem of cached information, virtual storage may not be compatible with all applications, and is not a panacea.

Modern operating systems utilize virtual memory systems that involve **swap files**. In order to offer users the ability to use more memory than is actually installed on a computer, portions of memory are, at times, stored to disk. The discussion of virtual memory and paging systems is beyond the scope of this book. What is important to realize is that even in a sophisticated SSL VPN environment in which the cached data is wiped or encrypted virtual storage spaces are used, it is possible that some sensitive data will be stored in a swap file and not properly eliminated after a user's session. That said, extracting such data is not trivial; it is extremely unlikely that a curious user will be able to do so.

However, in situations in which espionage attempts can be expected and in which professional attempts at extracting data may be made, it would be wise not to access sensitive resources from an untrusted computer.

The Problem: Third Party Search Tools Running on Access Devices

One security problem alluded to earlier is that third-party search tools (for example, Google Desktop Search Tool) running on computers used for accessing an SSL VPN may create cached versions of web pages and documents accessed during SSL VPN sessions.

Even SSL-encrypted pages may be stored in unencrypted form! This poses a serious security concern even for people using SSL VPNs that wipe temporary data after the completion of each SSL VPN session. Data cached by search tools—and index information created by such tools—may persist in the search-engine's proprietary data stores even after the aforementioned erasure. It may be difficult or impractical to erase the entire search-tool cache, and often it is impossible to remove individual records from the cache. In essence, search tools can create proprietary caches that may be effectively inaccessible to the SSL VPN.

The Solution

There are several ways of addressing this problem:

- **Block access**: The SSL VPN should block access if it detects search tools (or indexing tools) running on the access device. This will limit access, but will avoid caching of any data. Of course, the SSL would need to be aware of what search tools to look for and how to identify them.

- **Turn off indexing tool**: The SSL VPN should turn off the indexing tool, and restart it upon completion of the SSL VPN session. Again, this requires knowledge of the search tools.

- **Use removable encrypted virtual storage space**: The SSL VPN session should never store any unencrypted files on disk—instead it should use an encrypted virtual storage space that is removed after the session is completed. This approach does not require an understanding of how the search tools work. However, it may not protect against caching of data by all tools, and may not prevent sensitive data from being incorporated into the tool's index (even if the original copy of the data is inaccessible afterward to the index).

Department of Defense (DoD) Requirements

Erasing temporary information from access devices is not as simple as calling operating-system routines that delete the pertinent files. This is true for three reasons:

- Today's operating systems offer features that help prevent accidental erasure of important data. Among these features are 'Trash Can' or 'Recycle Bin' capabilities that actually move deleted files to a special folder in which they are stored until the space they occupy is needed for storing other files. Because files can be restored from these special folders and operating systems facilitate such recovery, SSL VPNs should not rely on calling operating system Delete commands to remove sensitive information from access devices.

- Even when a Trash Can/Recycle Bin is not used, operating systems typically do not fully erase files from disk when they are 'deleted'. Instead, they erase the references to the deleted files in the catalog of the disk's contents, so that the files are no longer accessible or officially 'taking up space' on the disk, even though their contents remain magnetically present until they are written over with new data. Until they are actually overwritten, files can easily be reconstructed after deletion using special software.

- Even when files are logically deleted from disk and overwritten with new data, the physical magnetic traces of the original information remains. By using sophisticated tools, people can sometimes recover erased data from magnetic media. To prevent such recovery, computers can write over the erased data several times with sequences of random 1s and 0s. With each subsequent writing onto a physical section of the disk, the previous data on the disk becomes increasingly difficult to recover.

The United States Department of Defense (specification 5220.22-M) sets criteria for properly erasing files that require at least three complete passes in order for information to be considered erased and unlikely to be retrieved. Some SSL VPNs today offer DoD-compliance erasure of temporary data when using one of the final two aforementioned methods of addressing temporary data.

The Problem: Users May Neglect to Log Out

It is an unfortunate reality that some users abandon computer sessions without properly logging out. This is especially true in web environments, in which a user may authenticate to a system and use it, but then browse another website and not realize that the original authenticated communications session remains live. Authenticated sessions that are left alive on deserted computers may be used by unauthorized parties for nefarious purposes and this can lead to severe consequences. This issue is not unique to SSL VPN technology—all web-based systems suffer from this vulnerability.

To combat the problem of abandoned sessions, web applications typically implement inactivity timeout systems. If they detect that there has been no activity by a user for some pre-defined period, they terminate the session as if the user logged out.

Such inactivity timeouts are clearly a necessity (even a fundamental element of SSL VPN security), which protects organizations against sessions being used by unauthenticated parties after legitimate users neglect to log off. However, implementing timeouts in an SSL VPN environment can be tricky due to the following issues:

- **An SSL VPN may inadvertently terminate legitimate user sessions and cause loss of work**: The problem stems from the fact that when users are entering information into a web browser form, they do not transmit any data to the SSL VPN server until they actively send it to the server by clicking on a Submit button. As a result, if a user is completing a long web form, the SSL VPN may not discover any user activity for some significant period of time. If the time period elapses before the user clicks Submit and the activity is received by the SSL VPN server only afterward, the user will get a message that he or she has been logged out of the SSL VPN. This will cause the user to lose whatever work was in progress on the form (and anywhere else in the SSL VPN session, for that matter). Practical ramifications of this issue include serious inconveniences for users completing long web forms and those composing long e-mail messages—both of whom may suffer an abruptly terminated session and loss of work.

- **Some non-activity may be detected as activity and abandoned sessions may not be appropriately terminated**: The flipside to the aforementioned problem is also true. Some applications offer an automatic refresh feature: that is, they periodically refresh the display of a web page in order to show the current information to the user. For example, popular e-mail packages may periodically refresh the user's view of the Inbox, and Personal Information Manager (PIM) applications may periodically refresh calendar views, etc. Although, automatic refresh is clearly a desirable feature, it does create issues when implementing timeouts. Automatic refresh capabilities function by adding code to web pages that cause web browsers to periodically poll a server for updated versions of the page; periodic requests automatically generated by web browsers, however, appear as user activity to SSL VPN servers. All the SSL VPN server knows is that data is being transmitted from the user's browser to the SSL VPN—a sign of user activity. As such, if applications sporting automatic refresh features are accessed via an SSL VPN, inactivity timeout security mechanisms may fail to operate, and abandoned sessions may remain live indefinitely. (This problem may also exist if an SSL VPN is used to establish a network-like connection over SSL and an automatic pinger or similar technology is used.)

- **User sessions may be misused before a timeout occurs**: Mischievous folks still have a window of opportunity during which they may abuse abandoned sessions before the prescribed inactivity threshold passes. Timeout systems based on a lack of activity wait for some period to elapse before terminating sessions. This allows a mischievous person to approach the access device before the necessary time period has elapsed, and use the session before a timeout occurs, thereby generating user activity, and completely undermining the effectiveness of the timeout system.

The Solution

Several technologies are used by SSL VPNs to address the aforementioned concerns:

Long Timeout Thresholds: Not a Good Idea

Before examining some appropriate mechanisms to address the aforementioned concerns, let us review one common approach that should not be followed.

One way that system administrators have defeated the problem of legitimate users being inconvenienced by inappropriate timeouts is by increasing timeout thresholds to much longer periods of time than users would normally expend on tasks such as completing forms and writing e-mails. Such an approach, however, is seriously flawed.

Allowing unattended sessions to remain live for long periods of time dramatically increases the chances of unauthorized users acquiring access during the period in which the session remains live on an abandoned computer. Effectively, long timeouts defeat the purpose for having timeouts in the first place.

Secondly, in a web environment a user may begin to work on a form or e-mail message and then browse through other websites, while planning to resume work on the original task at a later point. As such, there is no good measure as to how long it takes to write an e-mail message, and any guesses or estimates made will be inaccurate.

Of course, long timeout thresholds do nothing to address the issue of applications that support automatic-refresh capabilities.

In short, long timeout thresholds should not be used as a mechanism of addressing the aforementioned inconvenience as they exacerbate security concerns.

Non-Intrusive Timeout Systems

One appropriate way to address the problem of users neglecting to log out is by using non-intrusive timeouts.

Non-intrusive timeout systems are inactivity-based timeout systems where users are given warnings before a timeout occurs. Two thresholds are utilized—one for warning a user of an impending timeout, and one for actually terminating a user's session. For example, an SSL VPN may be configured to warn a user after eight minutes of inactivity that unless the system detects activity within the next two minutes, the session will be terminated. Coupled with the warning may be a button the user can click to generate such activity (for example, clicking OK to confirm receipt of the warning message). If the user does not respond to the message or generate server-noticeable activity, the session will be terminated after two minutes (i.e., after ten minutes expire with no activity).

Warnings can be delivered as pop-up windows that simply ask the user: Are you still there? with buttons that read Yes and No (or even just with a Yes button). If the user responds, the SSL VPN sees user activity and resets the inactivity timer's countdown. If the user does not respond within the prescribed period, the session is terminated.

Forced Periodic Re-Authentication

Forced Periodic Re-authentication (FPA) entails forcing an authenticated user to re-enter his or her credentials after some administrator-determined time window has elapsed, in order to continue working.

In addition to the previously mentioned threshold settings, an SSL VPN that supports FPA offers another security feature for dealing with users forgetting to log off—it requires users to re-enter the credentials periodically regardless of activity levels. When the prescribed time period elapses and a user is prompted for credentials, one of two situations result. If the user re-authenticates, the session resumes right where it left off, even if it was in the middle of completing a web form; if not, the session is terminated.

Although it is an imperfect solution, FPA is probably the best way to address the problem of unauthorized users gaining access to an SSL VPN session by approaching an abandoned access device and commencing usage before the prior abandoned session is timed out. FPA will not prevent the mischievous party from gaining access, as the SSL VPN has no way to distinguish the illegitimate user from the previous party using the computer until the FPA occurs. However, it will contain the damage by limiting the length of time for which the unauthorized party can use the session.

Ignoring Phony Activity

In order for timeout mechanisms to function properly in an environment in which computers generate automatic refresh requests or other traffic that is normally indistinguishable from user activity, the SSL VPN must have some mechanism by which it knows to process requests in auto-generated traffic but to ignore such traffic when determining when the last user activity transpired. This can be achieved by adding to the SSL VPN configuration a list of requests to be ignored when checking for user activity. In the case of web applications (which generate most of the problem) this is typically relatively simple; automatic refresh requests are usually sent as special URLs, and since there are typically only a limited number of such URLs per application, it is not difficult to create a list of these URLs. For non-web applications, defining what constitutes an automatic-refresh request can be a bit more complicated, but is certainly possible as the automatic requests typically exhibit characteristics that differ from true user activity.

Timeout Thresholds

As discussed earlier, it is imperative that SSL VPN administrators configure their SSL VPNs to utilize appropriate warning, timeout, and re-authentication thresholds. Some SSL VPNs come with default settings for these values, some are delivered without such settings, and some are even shipped without their timeout systems enabled. In any case, settings should be reset to conform to company policies.

The Problem: Viruses Enter Corporate Networks via the SSL VPN

One of the more obvious risks of allowing remote access from machines not under organizational control is the possibility of viruses being transferred from improperly managed computers to corporate networks. The ability to upload files to file systems from any computer greatly increases the chances that a file containing a virus will be deposited onto a computer on the corporate network from an infected computer. The threat of contamination is exacerbated by the fact that SSL VPNs offer remote access to e-mail, Customer Relationship Management (CRM) systems, and various other systems that allow users to attach files to messages or database entries, or otherwise upload files into a corporate database.

The Solution

There are several approaches taken to address the issue of viruses spreading via the SSL VPN. Three of the common strategies are:

- Check for use of antivirus technology on the client computer
- Block uploads
- Rely on internal network antivirus systems

Check for Anti-Virus Software on the User's Device

One increasingly common approach to preventing the spread of viruses to corporate networks via SSL VPN access is to have the SSL VPN server inspect each user's device for the presence of anti-virus software prior to allowing access to some or all of the functions of the SSL VPN. Checks can be performed to verify that anti-virus software is installed, running, using current signature databases, etc. People using computers that meet the criteria set by the organization are allowed access; those whose systems do not meet the necessary standards may be given access only to a subset of the systems offered by the SSL VPN, or may be prohibited from accessing altogether. If a user is blocked, the

SSL VPN may explain the reason for the denial of access as well as where to obtain the necessary software (or updates) to upgrade the client computer so as to be permitted to gain access.

Block Uploads

Another approach used to help prevent the spread of viruses to corporate networks over SSL VPN connections is to block users from uploading files to internal networks from remote computers. This blocking may be absolute and universal, or, as will be discussed in the Tiers of Access section, may be relaxed if the computer the user is using is adequately shielded from viruses.

Rely on Internal Network Antivirus

A third approach for preventing an SSL VPN from becoming a catalyst for the proliferation of viruses is to rely on previously existent antivirus technology on the corporate LAN to address the issue of viruses, with no new anti-virus technology implemented within the confines of the SSL VPN solution.

Files uploaded from an SSL VPN file-access window, for example, would be scanned on file servers to which they are added. Attachments to e-mail messages sent from an SSL VPN session would be subjected to anti-virus scanning performed on the e-mail server.

Although this approach theoretically handles all cases of virus, it suffers from several shortcomings. Viruses may be e-mailed as encrypted e-mail attachments (which will avoid detection by anti-virus software on the corporate network), or may be deposited onto an internal server and spread before the internal anti-virus system has the chance to detect and remove them. From a more general perspective, it is always better to prevent viruses from entering a network than to allow them to spread, then catch and delete them.

The Problem: Worms Enter Corporate Networks via the SSL VPN

Viruses and worms are often confused with one another, but they are not the same. Viruses are pieces of malicious code that attach themselves to some other code (a host) and are executed when the host code is run. Worms are independent programs that do not seek to attach themselves to other programs; instead, they reproduce across network connections.

The problem of worms being spread to corporate networks via the SSL VPN is therefore a different issue than that of viruses. Anti-virus systems may help block some worms, but because worms do not require human involvement in order to replicate, and because they replicate faster than viruses, they pose additional danger to SSL VPN implementations.

A worm that has compromised a computer used for accessing an SSL VPN may be able to exploit the SSL VPN connection to replicate to an organization's internal network. Because worms require no human interaction in order to spread, a device may be infected while connected to an SSL VPN session and within seconds of having become infected successfully infect numerous machines on the internal network. This may all happen before anti-virus software even detects the presence of the worm.

The Solution

Setting and enforcing a policy of not allowing access from machines not known to be safe would help alleviate the problem of worms spreading, but implementing such a rule can severely curtail the usability of SSL VPN and diminish the value of deploying it. However, it may be wise to prevent users accessing from machines not known to be secured against worms from establishing network-level connections over the SSL VPN. This will be discussed in detail later in this chapter.

In addition, it is important to discuss two technologies that can help prevent the spread of worms to corporate networks via an SSL VPN—personal firewalls and application firewalls. Although these two technologies have similar names, they are quite different:

Personal Firewalls

These are software packages installed on computers or handheld devices that manage communications to and from the systems upon which they are installed. Personal firewalls are configured with security policies, and permit or deny various types of communications based on these policies. As such, personal firewalls can serve as a good barrier against worms infecting user computers and against worms being able to spread outward from infected machines. SSL VPNs can check for the presence of a properly configured personal firewall on devices used for access; different SSL VPN access policies can be set based on whether such security technology is in place or not. (Some organizations may not allow any access if inadequate security is in place at the access device; others may allow limited access.)

Application Firewalls

These software packages or appliances sit in front of servers that serve content to Internet-based users. They offer reverse-proxying capabilities, but also filter users' requests to root out rogue instructions; they allow only valid activity to reach real servers. There are several technologies used in application firewalls and a high-level understanding is useful when developing an understanding of SSL VPN security.

Negative-Logic-Based Filtering of User Requests

Negative-logic filtering works in a fashion similar to basic anti-virus engines. It compares inbound requests with a set of signatures of known attacks; any requests that appear to match the signature of any known attack are blocked from reaching protected servers. Although negative-logic-based filtering is quite effective at preventing known attacks, it is not necessarily appropriate for use with SSL VPNs on its own, as it is powerless when it comes to shielding against newer attacks for which no signatures have yet been added to the signature database. Since zero day attacks (attacks based on new vulnerabilities for which no patches yet exist) are becoming increasingly common, this weakness is quite problematic. Negative logic also requires frequent maintenance attention as signature sets need to be updated on a regular basis for the system is to be effective.

Positive-Logic-Based Filtering

Positive-logic filtering works the other way round. Requests are all examined and compared against a set of signatures of valid requests—that is, of the types of communications that are supposed to be sent to specific protected servers. Any requests not conforming to the signature set are blocked. Positive-logic filtering requires more up-front investment than negative-logic (as filters must be enabled to identify appropriate and valid requests), but requires less maintenance than negative-logic systems, as signatures are not frequently updated. Additionally, positive logic can protect against zero-day attacks and new worms; attacks by definition cannot utilize valid requests and will not match the information contained in a properly configured signature set.

Dynamic-Rules-Based Filtering

Dynamic filtering technology involves dynamically scanning each outgoing web page at the filter as it is served, and establishing real-time policies as to what responses can be made by users based on what was sent. Users' responses are then subjected to positive-logic-like filtering to ensure they match an expected response. Sometimes the rules for static web pages are established ahead of time (which improves performance). Although optimal in theory, dynamic filtering suffers from several significant problems that render it impractical. For one, the processing required to examine web pages and deduce valid responses can result in a negative performance impact. In addition, it is difficult (if not impossible) to successfully generate proper rule-bases for today's complex applications on the fly, and a rule-set that is only 99% appropriate could block legitimate business activity or allow a successful security breach. There is also no Quality Assurance testing period for rules generated and implemented in real time. Any mistakes made during rule generation are immediately utilized as part of a production security system—a fact that could lead to potentially disastrous results.

Combination of Methods

Combinations of the aforementioned mechanisms can be used to gain the strengths of multiple methods without suffering from the weaknesses of any individual technique. For example, one could utilize positive-logic-based rules, but allow in those rules the inclusion of variables whose values are set dynamically during user sessions based on what is being accessed and who is requesting the access. Alternatively, positive logic can be used in conjunction with rules explicitly blocking known attacks. In the context of

SSL VPNs, application firewalling may take place on the SSL VPN server itself or on a proxy situated in front of the SSL VPN (more on this later in this chapter and in Chapter 5). In either case, the application firewall inspects requests sent by users, and before relaying any data to SSL VPN processing, subjects the incoming application-level data to stringent security checks.

Problems of Insecure Locations

Several other issues should be discussed pertaining to access from insecure locations. Some of these are relevant regardless of whether SSL VPN or some alternative remote-access technology is used, whereas others are specific to SSL VPN.

Spyware

Spyware refers to software installed without a user's knowledge to monitor a user's activity on a computer surreptitiously. The information that spyware gathers may be used to perpetrate crimes—say, pilfering credit card numbers and using them to make unauthorized purchases—or for unethical purposes—such as gathering on-line shopping preferences and using them to target advertisements and other marketing materials. In any event, it is clearly important to users accessing sensitive systems that their activities are not spied upon; yet, public and borrowed computers may not be immune to spyware. Some SSL VPNs can check for the presence of spyware on devices used for access, and some check for anti-virus packages that also detect spyware. Inspection for spyware however is typically based on signatures of known spyware and some heuristics, and is far from perfect (the checking technology is less mature than that of anti-virus engines). As such, some degree of caution should be exercised when accessing from machines that are likely candidates for spyware infection.

Keystroke Loggers

One way for mischievous parties to capture sensitive information from unsuspecting users is to utilize keystroke loggers on computers that their victims are using. There are two major forms of keystroke loggers in use today—hardware and software.

Hardware Keystroke Loggers

Hardware keystroke loggers are small devices that plug into a computer's keyboard port (or USB port if a USB keyboard is used) into which the keyboard is attached. The device, which usually looks like a little adapter or extension cable, records all of the keystrokes typed on the keyboard into a memory buffer. Ever so often, the party that installed the logger retrieves the logger from the device being spied upon, downloads the keystroke records to another computer, resets the logger, and reinstalls it onto the spied-on device.

The simplest method to combat hardware-based loggers is to examine any computer from which sensitive information will be accessed to see if such a device is installed. It is possible for someone to install such a logger on the inside of a computer—however, unless it is an inside job by someone working at an Internet Café or the like, such a scenario is not likely to occur in most environments. Of course, if extremely private information is being accessed, even such a risk is too great to take. As always, every risk must be evaluated against business needs and acceptable risk levels.

In any event, the problem of hardware-based keystroke loggers does bring to light the point that if data is extremely sensitive it probably should not be accessed remotely from any public location. This is true regardless of whether SSL VPN, IPSec VPN, or some other technology is used—as discussed below.

Software Keystroke Loggers

Software keystroke loggers are a form of spyware—they are software programs that record users' keystrokes and save them for retrieval by another party (or automatically forward the keystroke information to that party). They are addressed in a similar manner to other spyware as discussed above.

Shoulder Surfing

People have grown accustomed to protecting calling-card numbers from being seen by others when using them to make calls from telephones in public locations. Similar protection is required for sensitive data being accessed via an SSL VPN from any location where parties who are not authorized to see the information on the access device's display are present. It is a reasonable possibility that curious or mischievous parties lurking in public places may be able to read the contents of user's screens.

Video Cameras Aimed at Computers

The problem of shoulder surfing has grown as surveillance and security equipment has become increasingly inexpensive and ubiquitous. Cameras may capture the actions of anyone working in an airport, hotel lobby, or even in an outdoor park. As such, regardless of what type of remote-access technology is used (IPSec, SSL, etc.), the contents of one's screen should be carefully shielded from any monitoring devices. As surveillance equipment is sometimes disguised or otherwise obscured from view, extremely sensitive information should not be accessed in locations in which it is reasonable to expect such equipment to be present—even if the user does not actually detect the presence of such devices. As stated previously, the nature of one's business and the specific data being accessed should serve as the basis for determining what level of risk is acceptable.

Emanations

For the truly paranoid and for those people who utilize extremely sensitive information on a regular basis, it is worth mentioning the issue of **emanations**. When electronic devices are used, they emit electromagnetic radiation. Government standards (that vary between nations) govern the levels of emanations that are considered acceptable, but just because a particular level of emanation is safe for people, does not mean that it is safe for data protection. In fact, by using sophisticated equipment someone could intercept emanations from computer equipment and spy and extract various information about activities transpiring on the system.

There are technologies that can insulate computer equipment from such eavesdropping (in the US, insulating equipment that meets such requirements is known as TEMPEST-compliant), but, Internet kiosks in public locations and most borrowed computers are obviously not shielded in such a fashion. Neither are corporate-owned laptops when used in public locations. As such, it is possible for someone utilizing specialized (and expensive) equipment to spy on users of such machines even without shoulder surfing or using a video camera. So, military-type secrets or other extremely sensitive information that mischievous parties would be willing to expend significant resources to obtain should not be accessed from machines not known to be protected against emissions in any location in which someone could be spying on the equipment.

Hackers Bridging to the Corporate Network

Another risk posed by SSL VPN access is that an unauthorized party may gain access to a corporate network by bridging to it through the SSL VPN user's computer. A user's computer is often connected to a local network. Simultaneously, when the user is accessing an SSL VPN session, the computer may be networked to a remote corporate network. The computer is therefore simultaneously connected to two networks. It may be therefore possible for someone using one network—in our case the network local to the user's computer—to connect to the corporate network via the dual-homed machine and the SSL VPN.

Furthermore, there is also some degree of risk for the local network that the user is connected to—a system on the SSL VPN server's network may be able to connect to it via the SSL VPN tunnel. This is not a threat to the organization providing the SSL VPN access, but may prove a liability for the firm if the SSL VPN is abused in such a fashion. Furthermore, this problem may give organizations just cause to prohibit users from establishing SSL VPN connections from their equipment (to SSL VPNs run by other entities) unless the other entities do not allow network-level connectivity. This is similar to the situation that currently exist vis-à-vis IPSec VPN technology.

The Problem: Internal Networking Information may be Leaked

Hackers preparing to attack a network typically try to map out its resources in an effort to determine which attack techniques would prove most effective. An understanding of internal machine names, directory structures, IP addresses, and the like, can be invaluable to a hacker and greatly assist him or her in breaching system security.

Unfortunately, SSL VPNs are often culpable for providing such information to outside parties. As described in Chapter 3, one of the functions of an SSL VPN is to translate internal resource information to an externally accessible format. Although such a translation would seem to obscure any internal information from external parties, the reality is that some SSL VPNs generate externally accessible URLs, but pass the internal information needed to reconstruct the true destination address as a clear-text parameter (or within the URL as a "directory"). The parameter, which contains valuable internal information, can be read by anyone watching the SSL VPN session. Sometimes even the user himself should never be afforded with information about the internal infrastructure. This is especially true if partners, customers, or prospects will utilize the SSL VPN.

The Solution

The solution to this problem is quite simple—mature SSL VPN technology does not pass internal information in clear-text to remote parties. The information is either embedded as part of the URL in an encrypted form, passed as an encrypted parameter, or stored on the SSL VPN server and referenced with some code number added to the URL sent to users. Other schemes may be used as well—the point is to hide internal network architecture information from external users.

Printing and Faxing

Users utilizing an SSL VPN may wish to print on local printers (i.e., printers located where they are working) or may want to print on remote printers located in their office (local to the SSL VPN). Security concerns of these types of printing include:

Printers Local to the User

Two concerns with regard to users printing on local printers are:

1. If a shared printer is used, it is possible that another user will see the printout (or even retrieve the printout) before the user does. Sensitive information may be obtained by unauthorized parties in such a fashion, and, if the other party reads the document without actually stealing it, the user may never know that such information was seen by an outsider.

2. Today's operating systems typically spool data before sending it to the printer—they store an image of what is to be printed to disk and then transfer that image to the printer rather than have applications communicate directly with the printer. Although spooling makes the printing experience much more efficient (printers can easily be shared) and user-friendly (as users can get back to work even before the actual printing occurs), it creates some security concerns. With regard to SSL VPN the problem is that if sensitive information is printed, it is contained within a spooled image that is stored on a machine not under organizational control. The user may not know who has access to the spooled image or where it is stored. As such, it is sometimes

wise to disable spooling when printing sensitive information accessed during an SSL VPN session.

Printers Local to the SSL VPN Server

Clearly, spooling poses no problems when one uses an SSL VPN from within the confines of one's office. (If the spooling within the office is not secure, then there is a serious problem for all users, not just for SSL VPN users.) However, the issue of printing on printers within the office when a user is actually remote is a serious issue. The user who is doing the printing cannot see who is standing near the printer and simply does not know who in the office will actually retrieve the printout. As such, although there are appropriate uses for such remote printing, care should be exercised when performing such an operation.

Deleted Files

Another area in which operating system functions can affect the security of an SSL VPN session is in terms of deletion of data.

In many situations files that users actively copy from remote drives (or from anywhere else) to a local machine will not be erased when users complete their SSL VPN sessions and so users must be sure to delete these files.

As described earlier with regard to the erasure of temporary data upon session termination, today's operating systems do not typically fully erase data when the user erases it. Rather, they utilize special folders to hold the data until the physical location of the data is needed for other purposes. As described earlier, even when the files are overwritten erasure is not complete. To erase the data completely, the user must actually write over the space on disk several times. This is not always easily achieved; but then, this level of security is often not necessary. The much greater risk for an average user is that a curious party will look for files in a computer's Trash Bin folder—not that someone will try to restore data using specialized hardware.

Trusted Endpoint

SSL VPNs offer organizations the ability to configure some computers to be considered trusted; users utilizing such devices for access may be granted access to more resources than they would be allowed to access from general systems. **Trusted devices** are typically corporate owned and managed computers, and are sometimes known as **managed devices**. When trusted devices are used, certain security routines may not be needed—for example, temporary files need not be erased from corporate laptops on which numerous sensitive files (e.g., business documents) are intentionally stored. Timeout thresholds should be different when users are using devices to which only they have access as opposed to when people use a computer in an Internet Café.

Client certificates are often used to identify computers that should be trusted. SSL VPN administrators issue special and unique client certificates for each machine that the SSL VPN will trust and these certificates are installed on the appropriate user devices. Although such certificates are often installed by administrators themselves, SSL VPNs can allow users to request such certificates online, and provide for the automatic download and installation of such certificates once an administrator has approved a user's request.

Advanced trusted endpoint capabilities include the ability to scan access devices for information other than client certificates that may also be useful in determining trust levels—for example, checking for the presence of a special USB drive with specific contents, a specific software package with a special configuration, or a previously configured registry key set to a specific value. Such a scan may be performed in lieu of, or in combination with, the check for an appropriate client certificate. Of course, different levels of trust may exist with different policies, based on those trust levels.

Tiers of Access Based on Endpoint Situation

SSL VPNs are accessed from computers of differing natures—company-owned laptops, home computers, public Internet kiosks, handheld devices, etc. All of these different machines offer different levels of security and trust; access rights from these devices should not always be uniform. For example, it is not wise to allow file uploads from a machine that is likely to be infected with viruses; but such uploads may be safe from a corporate laptop known to have anti-virus software running on it. So, what level of access should an SSL VPN provide if access is to be gained from diverse devices?

The simplest method to address access in a scenario of differing trust levels is to utilize a *lowest common denominator approach*—that is, to provide only access that is safe to offer from all machines. However, such an approach severely compromises the return on investment achievable by implanting an SSL VPN as it curtails access unnecessarily from machines from which access need not be limited.

It is clearly ideal, therefore, not to take such a limiting approach with regard to SSL VPN access, and instead, to identify the security level of access devices and institute session-specific access policies accordingly. The maximum level of access that can be securely offered from a particular device should be delivered to the user when using that device.

Corporate security policies governing access devices normally dictate conditions in order to permit users to perform specific business functions. In our previous example, a policy would dictate that uploads may only be done from devices running proper anti-virus software. SSL VPNs should be configured to fully implement such policies and block access to specific applications or portions of applications if security policies so dictate.

The level of access allowed for a particular session is normally determined when a user logs in. A small applet sent to the access device examines it, determining how the device meets various criteria previously set by the SSL VPN administrators based on corporate security policies. It may also attempt to install various security-related code onto the access device and report back to the SSL VPN server on its success. Based on the applet's findings, the security level for the device is set and access controls are implemented accordingly. Alternatively, pre-packaged software utilities previously installed on an access device may perform the checking. The process of checking the security environment of an access device is sometimes known as **Host Integrity Checking** or **Access Device Integrity Checking**.

It is important to note that access controls may limit functionality within an application, not just limit access to an application in its entirety. One common example of this is expressed in the following self-explanatory chart that shows a sensible policy regarding e-mail access from devices with various security conditions:

Condition at Access Device			Access Controls			
Trusted Machine	**Anti-Virus Present**	**Ability to erase temporary files**	**Allow user to read e-mail (text messages)**	**Allow user to send e-mail (text messages)**	**Allow user to open e-mail attachments**	**Allow user to send e-mail attachments**
No	Yes	Yes	Yes	Yes	Yes	Yes
No	Yes	No	Yes	Yes	No	Yes
No	No	Yes	Yes	Yes	Yes	No
No	No	No	Yes	Yes	No	No
Yes – Trust Level 2	Yes	Yes/No	Yes	Yes	Yes	Yes
Yes – Trust Level 2	No	Yes/No	Yes	Yes	Yes	No
Yes – Trust Level 1	Yes/No	Yes/No	Yes	Yes	Yes	Yes

Factors affecting what level of access a user will be provided may include:

- **Anti-virus software**: Is it running? Which anti-virus product is being used? What is the version of the software? How old are the signatures?

- **Personal Firewall**: Is it running? Which personal firewall product is being used? What is the version of the software? What policies are in effect?

- **Authentication Mechanism**: A user who supplies a username and password combination may be given access to fewer resources than one who uses a one-time password, plugs a special USB token into the computer during authentication, etc.

- **Operating System**: What operating system is the user's computer using?

- **Registry Keys**: Are specific key values set?

- **Client Certificates**: Is one present? What does it signify?

- **Patch Levels**: Which OS and other system patches are installed?

- **IP address of the user's device**: Some IP addresses may be trusted (e.g., if they are on the internal network).

> Trusting IP addresses is not a great idea as they can be spoofed, internal IP numbering schemes may be identical in multiple environments, and computers protected by proxies may appear to SSL VPN servers to be using the proxies' addresses.

- **Internet Provider**: Is the user using a preferred provider that offers various security functionalities while connecting?

- **Anti-spyware packages**: Are any running? Which ones?

- **Temporary files**: Can the SSL VPN's temporary files delete routine run on this machine?

> When access is achieved from trusted devices much of the security and access technology may already be present before the user logs in. When users use public or borrowed computers, the SSL VPN will typically need to send all of the code to the user's machine—this is sometimes referred to as delivering the software **'on demand'**.

Internet Provider Controls

For both economic and security reasons, organizational policies often mandate that users perform all remote access connectivity through specific telecommunications providers. Such providers may offer discounted connection rates for large customers, or offer enforcement of specific policies (such as filtering out pornography and other potentially objectionable material or blocking the use of the connection for peer-to-peer file sharing). Some SSL VPN technologies can examine user-connection attributes, user IP addresses, and pertinent routing information and block users who are not utilizing the requisite Internet provider from accessing corporate resources via the SSL VPN.

Server-Side Security Issues

Now that we have explored the various issues pertinent to client-side security, let us examine the significant server-side security risks that must be addressed when implementing an SSL VPN. Server-side security includes issues related to both protecting the internal network from compromises made possible by the presence of the SSL VPN and the access it offers, and protection of the SSL VPN server itself.

The Problem: Firewalls and Other Security Technologies may be Undermined

For Internet-based users to communicate with the SSL VPN, and for the SSL VPN to be able to relay requests to internal systems, communications must transpire utilizing TCP/IP (and perhaps UDP/IP and ICMP as well). Firewalls, which block communications ports, must be configured to allow the communications required by the SSL VPN, but doing so poses serious risks. Let us examine the two most common scenarios to gain a better understanding of the problems that arise.

In a security-conscious organization, the SSL VPN server will not sit outside the shield of protection of the organization's perimeter firewall; it will be placed either within a (DMZ) or on an internal network.

SSL VPN in a DMZ

If the SSL VPN is located in a DMZ, the exterior firewall will have to allow port 443 (and probably also port 80) to be open for outside traffic including requests from users to flow to the SSL VPN. That in itself may not seem like a terrible risk as opening ports to web servers is done universally. However, in the case of SSL VPN, there is a real problem with doing so. The following figure shows an SSL VPN situated in a DMZ. This architectural scheme poses some security risks.

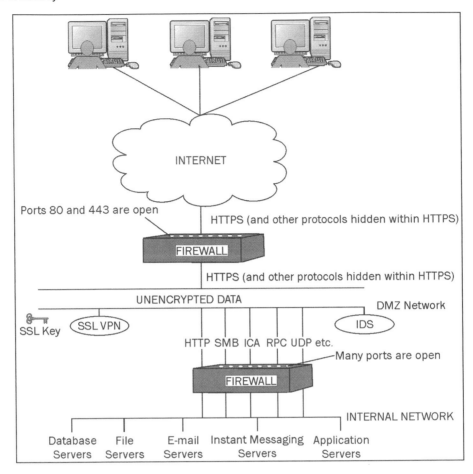

Because the SSL VPN tunnels various protocols through the external firewall and rebuilds them in the DMZ:

- **SSL decryption keys are maintained in an unsafe environment (the DMZ)**: If SSL keys are compromised, attackers may be able to impersonate the organization. Criminals who utilize phishing to steal sensitive information from users would love to obtain corporate SSL keys. Placing such keys in an un-trusted or semi-trusted location is not wise.

- **Decryption is performed in an insecure area (the DMZ)**: Communication of sensitive information occurs as plaintext (not encrypted) on the insecure DMZ network where it may be subject to sniffing and pilfering. As such, in this architectural scheme the SSL VPN does not afford true end-to-end encryption—it delivers end-to-middle encryption, as the contents of the SSL session are decrypted in an insecure location outside the destination network.

- **The exterior firewall is undermined by the SSL VPN**: If a remote user is allowed to establish network connectivity over SSL, then he or she can transmit essentially any desired protocol in network packets that are tunneled within HTTPS to the SSL VPN. This means that protocols that are supposed to be blocked by the exterior firewall slip by as they are tunneled (i.e., hidden) within HTTPS to the DMZ. When administrators configure the exterior firewall to block a specific port so as to disable use of a particular service from the Internet, they want that service blocked. Allowing such protocols to sneak in is likely to violate organizational security policies. (This is true even if the only users who are able to perform tunneling are authorized users.)

- **Numerous ports would need to be opened in the interior firewall**: This would enable inappropriate types of communications between the DMZ and the internal network. Opening such ports compromises the effectiveness of the interior firewall, blends the DMZ and Internet environments, and introduces serious security concerns. Additionally, opening such ports typically violates corporate security policies.

- **The remote node could serve as a bridge to another network**: If a remote user is allowed to establish a network-type connection over SSL, it is possible that anyone on that user's local network will be able to connect to the internal network via the access device used to access the SSL VPN. This poses a great threat to an organization's corporate infrastructure.

- **External parties could be allowed to become nodes on organizational networks**: Most security-conscious organizations prohibit any computer not belonging to the organization from becoming a node on the organization's network. If an SSL VPN is used for partners, customers, and prospects to access corporate resources and if the SSL VPN allows remote users to establish network connectivity over SSL, this policy will be violated (and the risks the policy seeks to mitigate will pose a serious threat).

SSL VPN on the Internal Network

Because of these risks, one might consider placing the SSL VPN server on the internal network and not in the DMZ. However, such a scheme also presents serious problems.

The following figure shows an SSL VPN situated on an internal network, which poses serious risks different from those created by utilizing the DMZ-based model:

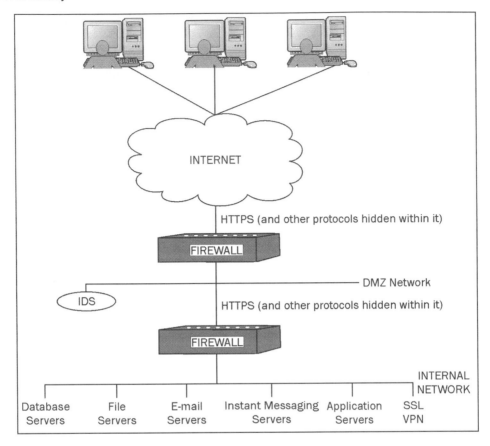

- **The entire firewall infrastructure is undermined**: Protocols that the firewalls are supposed to block are tunneled within SSL all the way to the internal network. By the time the SSL VPN server reconstitutes the native communication formats, the contents of those communications are already on the internal network—where they do not belong!

- **Unauthenticated parties are able to send network packets to the internal network**: Packets must be sent by remote users to the internal network in order to authenticate. Allowing such access violates standard corporate security policies, and, for good reason. Hackers and worms should not have any level of access to corporate resources. Offering them such access can lead to **Denial of Service (DoS)** attacks, mapping of the corporate network, or scanning for vulnerabilities that can be leveraged to pilfer data or commandeer control over computers.

- **Any network-based Intrusion Detection Systems (IDSs) present on the DMZ will be rendered ineffective**: IDSs work by scanning network packets as they traverse a network; placing IDSs on a DMZ is a good technique for stopping rogue traffic from entering a corporate network. However, in the case of an SSL VPN on the internal network, all requests are encrypted with SSL—if the requests traverse the DMZ in an encrypted form, the IDSs will not be able to read them. IDSs will, therefore, likely be unable to distinguish between valid user activity and even the most severe of attacks.

The Solution

There is no one simple solution to the aforementioned problems. However, using sensible approaches combined with proper use of technology can mitigate all of the previously mentioned problems.

An SSL VPN server must ensure that it properly integrates with and complements corporate firewalls in order to be safely incorporated into corporate infrastructure. Because of the aforementioned problems, using SSL as a tunneling mechanism for a true network connection is, generally speaking, problematic.

Establishment of a network connection over SSL should only be done for machines that you would allow onto your corporate network i.e., corporate-owned computers. Even when allowing secure machines to access in such a fashion, it is critical to realize that the personal firewalls on those computers are in effect transformed into perimeter firewalls for your organization, a task which they may not be equipped to do. So, establishing a network connection over SSL (which is certainly a powerful capability of SSL VPN technology) may not be ideal from a security standpoint.

Thankfully, establishing a network connection over SSL is not always necessary (and certainly not always recommended).

It is possible to achieve access to applications and files without establishing a network-level connection. As described in Chapter 3, requests to ports can be intercepted and tunneled, or network-related functions within the client device's operating system can be leveraged. Allowing access, without actually issuing an internal IP address to an endpoint device, is usually a much safer alternative to tunneling network information and mitigates many of the problems discussed above.

Furthermore, if only the upper layers of the OSI model are actually transferred to the SSL VPN (i.e., without creating a network node out of the remote device), then it is possible to have the regular firewall infrastructure perform network-level security and the SSL VPN perform application-level security. The SSL VPN can check to ensure that only specific application protocols are used, and that only requests that properly conform to those protocols are allowed to pass.

Granular controls that further refine access can be implemented. For example:

- Who can access (e.g., Authenticated username: JosephSteinberg)
- Which applications (e.g., Telnet)

- On which servers (e.g., Server 1)
- From which devices (e.g., from trusted computers and computers with personal firewalls and anti-virus programs on them)

A few good options to address storage of SSL Certificates in an insecure location are:

- The use of an SSL Accelerator, which would allow the SSL Certificate to be stored in the secure environment of the accelerator
- The use of Air Gap technology, explained later, which would allow relocation of the Certificate to the internal network protected by the Air Gap
- The use of Air Gap technology in conjunction with an SSL accelerator, which leverages the security of both technologies to protect the certificate

The Problem: Application-Level Vulnerabilities

Vulnerabilities in server software have received a significant amount of press coverage over the past few years. Holes in various products have led to the mass proliferation of worms, and have caused billions of dollars in damage worldwide.

Most SSL VPNs utilize web servers as part of their underlying architecture. As such, any vulnerability in the underlying web servers (or anywhere else within the SSL VPN software) may lead to a serious security breach. Even **hardening** (which is the process of optimizing a system's configuration in order to make it more secure) an SSL VPN appliance may not adequately address this problem; hardening is never perfect, and even hardened SSL VPN platforms have been found to suffer from vulnerabilities. In addition, vulnerabilities that may be present in an appliance's underlying operating system can completely undermine its security.

Even if the SSL VPN appliance itself remains secure, because it sends user requests to internal servers, vulnerabilities in internal systems may be exploited by sending attacks to the SSL VPN server, which, even if it itself is not compromised, will then relay the requests (i.e., the attacks) to internal servers.

The Solution

To prevent your SSL VPN implementation from falling prey to worms, it is imperative that application-level filtering be performed. Filtering may either be done through the use of a third-party product installed on a proxy sitting in front of the SSL VPN as shown in the diagram below (data flows in the order A,B,C,D,E) or may be integrated with and incorporated into the SSL VPN server itself.

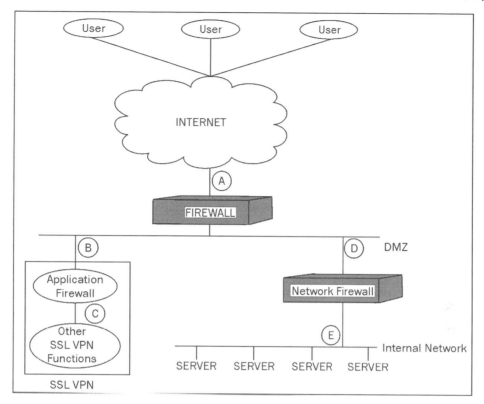

Filtering requests sent to the SSL VPN either as a function of the actual SSL VPN server or as a function of an application-level firewall situated in front of the SSL VPN can help address the problem of application-level vulnerabilities. Various types of filtering are discussed earlier in this chapter and, together, they can block rogue requests from crippling the SSL VPN, or from being able to reach and adversely affect internal systems.

Encryption

Proper encryption is essential whenever confidential information is transmitted across the Internet. In the case of SSL VPNs, SSL is the technology utilized to encrypt all communications. Today, with the proliferation of web browsers supporting 128-bit SSL encryption, and with relaxed export restrictions from the United States, there is little reason for most organizations not to take advantage of the strong 128-bit protection afforded by SSL. For more information on this topic please refer to Chapter 3 which discusses SSL in detail.

Patching of SSL VPN Servers

One point that should be made when discussing SSL VPN security is that no software product (or appliance-running software) is perfect. Bugs—some of which may create security vulnerabilities—are present in virtually all software packages produced today. SSL VPNs are not immune to programmer error; SSL VPN products may contain bugs that need to be fixed through the application of patches. Each SSL VPN product has its own story when it comes to patches—some products have historically required more patching than others, some offer positive-logic application firewalling technology within the SSL VPN server that reduces the need to rely on patching, whereas some utilize third-party products and rely on third-party patches in addition to their own.

Linux versus Windows

Today's SSL VPN servers typically run on either Microsoft Windows Server or variants of the Linux operating system. Although Microsoft has received a great deal of negative media coverage with regard to the security of it's operating system and software products, the reality is that all operating systems suffer from vulnerabilities, and Linux has also been proven to suffer from numerous deficiencies.

As Linux has matured and become industry-recognized as a viable platform for business systems, it has been subjected to a great deal more testing than in previous years; the tests performed, coupled with increased hacker attempts to compromise Linux boxes, have resulted in an increased concentration of vulnerabilities being found in Linux.

There has been an ongoing debate among technology professionals and enthusiasts as to whether Linux is more secure than Windows or vice versa and this debate will certainly not be settled in this book. What is important to understand is that neither Linux nor Windows should be considered a solid, impenetrable platform. All operating environments have bugs and vulnerabilities. Organizations considering deploying an SSL VPN should not view either platform as likely to withstand attacks on its own; relying on either option to be innately secure may result in disaster. Instead, organizations should consider the platform of SSL VPN appliances in relation to other systems in their data centers—if they already are utilizing many Linux-based systems then the management of an additional Linux box may be relatively simple; if they are using Microsoft systems then a Windows-based SSL VPN may make more sense from a management standpoint. It is important to remember that perhaps the most critical element in a security infrastructure is that human errors do not occur and having SSL VPN administrators utilize an operating environment with which they are already familiar will greatly reduce the chances of mistakes. In any case, additional security should be added to the boxes as described in the next section.

Some Other SSL VPN Appliance Security Concepts

SSL VPN servers serve as gateways from an Internet full of hostile marauders into the protected environments of corporate infrastructures. As such, they must offer solid defenses against attacks including mechanisms to ensure that they themselves remain resilient, fortified barriers. In addition to the technologies already discussed, several interesting concepts regarding solidification of SSL VPN servers re covered in the following sections.

Hardening

Hardening refers to the process of optimizing the configuration of a computer or network to make it as secure as possible. It usually entails disabling unnecessary services, modifying operating system defaults, disabling unnecessary networking capabilities, eliminating access rights for all users other than those who absolutely need to manage the device, and removing all unnecessary software. Many SSL VPNs are shipped on pre-hardened computers, sometimes called **appliances** (as was discussed earlier). Hardening certainly reduces the susceptibility of an SSL VPN to attack, and is an economical method of solidifying an SSL VPN platform. However, it is important to realize that hardening does not offer total resilience; if there is a flaw in the underlying operating system code, all the hardening procedures in the world may prove meaningless.

Air Gap

Air Gap is a technology that utilizes two servers—one that faces the internal world and upon which all of the SSL VPN functionality runs, and one that faces the Internet. Between them, there is a small memory bank. The externally facing server is hardened and only runs code that allows it to receive IP connections. It deposits the application payload from the packets it receives onto the memory bank from which the internal server reads the inbound requests. Air Gap offers stronger security than simple hardening as it eliminates network connectivity, reduces the risk of OS-level vulnerabilities being exploited, and prevents any Internet-connected machine from addressing the SSL VPN. The SSL VPN functionality as well as the SSL VPN server's security engine remain safe from tampering. Even if the externally facing server were breached by a hacker, no unauthorized access to the internal network would be available. On the other hand, if a simple hardened SSL VPN were compromised, it could be used as a staging ground for attacks against internal resources. One drawback of Air Gap is that it can make an SSL VPN deployment more expensive than simple hardening due to the need for dual servers. As such, Air Gap is typically better suited for larger implementations; in such situations security is typically paramount and the cost of an extra server is negligible in relation to the cost of overall SSL VPN project.

Protection from Internal Systems and the Internal Network

The SSL VPN server should be protected from tampering by internal users. Passwords should be required to access any of its administrative utilizes. Furthermore, it is useful to have some basic firewall capabilities on the SSL VPN server to help contain any worms or other malware that may be present on the internal network and block their spread to the SSL VPN server (which could become a catalyst for spreading them to remote users).

ASIC

Application-Specific Integrated Circuits (ASICs) are chips designed to run specific applications. They are common in cars and various electronic devices, and are now appearing in some SSL products including SSL VPNs. If security functions are incorporated into ASIC chips, the chips can improve the execution of web security functions, and may reduce the likelihood of the SSL VPN itself being compromised with certain types of attacks.

Summary

In this chapter, we have explored SSL VPN security. We discussed:

- Authentication, Authorization, and Single Sign On
- End-Point Security Concerns
- Trusted Endpoints and Tiered Access
- Server-Side Security Issues
- The need of patching for SSL VPN servers to remain resilient to attack
- Whether Windows or Linux is a more suitable SSL VPN server platform
- Some other miscellaneous topics related to SSL VPN security

In the next chapter, we will discuss how to plan for an SSL VPN implementation. We will cover the items to be considered before selecting a product, as well as how to prepare your IT infrastructure for the inclusion of SSL VPN technology.

5

Planning for an SSL VPN

SSL VPN certainly offers exciting potential but this does not mean that it is a perfect technology or that it is suitable for addressing every remote-access need. In this chapter, we will examine scenarios that are appropriate candidates for an SSL VPN deployment, and cases where IPSec or some other alternative technology might be better suited. We will also cover some important things to look for when selecting an SSL VPN product, and some guidelines for performing the actual preparation for SSL VPN implementation.

Determining Business Requirements

Technology is a tool that can be used to help people achieve business goals; as such, specific technology selections should always be based on business requirements and not vice versa. It is critical to define what objectives an organization wishes to address and based on such requirements, select an appropriate technical tool. The case of SSL VPNs is no exception to this rule.

Remote Access Paradigms

Remote Access needs often encompass two major categories of communications—Site-to-Site and User-to-Site.

- **Site-to-Site**: Organizations with multiple locations often want to merge multiple remote networks into what appears to be one big network. Rather than paying for expensive private links between various sites, companies can use VPN technology to create secure communication channels over the Internet and thereby link their various offices together. VPN connectivity between the Local Area Networks at each location is often implemented by means of special software installed on the perimeter firewalls at each site and is known as **Site-to-Site VPN** or **Firewall-to-Firewall VPN**. IPSec technologies are ideal for such connectivity—IPSec has been used for such connections for several years. SSL VPN vendors have not yet concentrated their efforts on such communication needs, and today's SSL VPN technology is not geared toward addressing Site-to-Site communications needs. Companies looking to implement Site-to-Site connectivity should opt for an alternative technology.

- **User-to-Site:** Remote access for users to corporate resources such as files, applications, databases, and terminal services, discussed in this book until this point, is commonly known as User-to-Site connectivity. SSL VPN technology is often an excellent choice when organizations are posed with User-to-Site requirements.

Now let us discuss how to prepare for an SSL VPN implementation to address User-to-Site needs.

Determining User Needs

SSL VPNs are a potential fit for User-to-Site remote access. But what access do users need when they are not physically located in an organization's facility? There is no one simple answer to this question.

Different Scenarios

Remote access needs vary by user and by group. Some technical users working in the MIS department of a large corporation may require network-level access from wherever they are located so that they can *ping* machines, while a sales representative simply wants remote access to web-based e-mail and the organizational CRM system. The functionality an enterprise needs and even the type of product an organization deploys is heavily dependent on the purposes for which the users will use it. The following are some common scenarios and suggested high-level implementation guidelines:

- **Full network-level access**: If business needs dictate that the only group of users needing remote access need to gain full network-level access as if they were in the office and access will only be performed from trusted corporate-owned computers, a low-end SSL-based solution may be appropriate. Some such solutions may even be free (at least in terms of initial layout), as firewall/IPSec VPN vendors are starting to offer SSL access of this nature as an add-on to existing infrastructure components.

- **Remote access to e-mail**: If general users need remote access to e-mail but not to other applications, an e-mail-specific solution may be an appropriate option. Several vendors offer such products and they usually cost significantly less than a full SSL VPN. (Usually, if the organization's needs grow, such solutions can be upgraded to a full SSL VPN.)

- **Access to multiple applications**: If users will need access to multiple applications and/or files, an SSL VPN of the nature described throughout this book should be considered.

- **Full remote network connectivity for a few remote users**: If only a small number of remote users need remote access, and they are highly technical individuals and require full remote network connectivity, an IPSec VPN may be the ideal option. A low-end SSL VPN that can establish such connectivity may also be appropriate.

- **Remote access from a small number of designated computers**: If remote access will be made available from only a small number of designated computers, either an IPSec VPN or an SSL VPN requiring client certificates for authentication may be a good option. (The SSL VPN is probably a better fit if the users are not highly technical.)

- **Access platform for e-business**: If the SSL VPN will serve as an access platform for not only employees but also e-business—in which case unauthenticated prospects and customers may need access to specific sections, an SSL VPN that supports such capabilities (application-level access, application firewalling, and so on) should be considered.

- **Multiple business requirements**: If multiple business requirements such as providing an employee remote-access portal and an e-business access platform must be serviced simultaneously, an SSL VPN capable of providing multiple independent SSL VPN portals should be considered.

- **Remote access to desktop machines for one or two users**: If remote access is only needed for one or two users and remote access to their desktop machines is sufficient then a product such as GoToMyPC, pcAnywhere, or a similar inexpensive product should be considered in lieu of an SSL VPN.

There are, of course, infinite possibilities as to business requirements. Each individual organization must weigh its needs versus the capabilities of the offerings available at the time of the need, as well as against expectations of future technological developments of the specific product types it is considering utilizing as a solution. In other words, it is important to consider how well any potential solution supports current business needs, how well it will support future business needs, and how well future versions of the product will support future business needs.

One important fact to remember when determining requirements is that users often do not understand what their own technical requirements are, but they usually do know what their business needs are. So, while a user may think that he or she needs network-type access to a system because that is how it has always been accessed in the past, it is possible that the application can be delivered without establishing a network connection. As such, while polling users to determine business needs, it is important to maintain independence from any technology suitable for providing potential solutions. In other words, find out what tasks users need to perform remotely and not how they think such access can be delivered.

Entire books have been written on methodologies for gathering business requirements, and they are not addressed further in this work. We will, however, examine several requirements that are often overlooked when planning for an SSL VPN.

Selecting an Appropriate SSL VPN

An SSL VPN is a strategic investment and investing in one demands proper attention to be paid to the selection of an appropriate product. Today, the official feature sets of most major SSL VPN products seem to have begun to converge. This leads some people to form an initial impression that the major distinction between the various products is the label on the front of the appliances. This, however, is most definitely not the case. Much as feature matrixes may look similar in marketing collaterals and on vendor websites, the nature of the underlying technology used by the various products often introduces substantial differences between the offerings. The strengths and weaknesses of each product must be compared against the business requirements of an organization before considering deployment and an appropriate solution should be selected accordingly.

Of course, it is also essential to factor in the solvency and trustworthiness of the vendor offering each solution; you may not want to do business with a company about to go bankrupt or which is undergoing a criminal investigation by government authorities. It is also important to realize that while consistency of vendors throughout a data center can sometimes simplify management, reliance on a small number of providers may also weaken security by increasing the ramifications of a single vulnerability.

In the following sections, we will cover several significant, but often overlooked, factors that organizations should consider when planning to deploy an SSL VPN. Although not all elements apply to all organizations, those that are pertinent to a particular environment may be critical in determining the success or failure of the SSL VPN effort.

Ensuring Proper Level of Access

It is obviously important to ensure that a product selected for deployment can actually deliver the type of access that is necessary. It is important to verify that the applications and functions that you need to work remotely with:

- Actually work via the SSL VPN
- Fully work via the SSL VPN (e.g., all functions within an application work)
- Work via the SSL VPN from the types of devices you expect users to use
- Work at the level you require them to (e.g., at the application level so they can be used securely from untrusted devices)

In other words, it is critical to ensure that the SSL VPN product can deliver what you need it to.

Many SSL VPNs offer all of the features that you need, but may not allow the combination of those features to work as you require. For example, an SSL VPN may allow applications to be accessed at the application level, and may allow file access, but may not allow file access at the application level. It is important to verify that the feature combinations that you require can be delivered by products you consider for deployment.

As mentioned above, it is essential that business needs be gathered without regard for the technology that will be used to address those needs. One often-overlooked area where this holds true is with regard to access control within applications. A particular application may be available to authorized users when they are physically situated in their offices, but such access may not be appropriate (as per security policies) when the same users are remote. Sometimes, access may be appropriate—but only to specific portions of the application. Sometimes access should be delivered to the application, but some functions within the application should be crippled. In fact, as discussed in Chapter 4, several tiers of access may be necessary in order to enforce security policies properly. If your policies dictate that access should be tiered, make sure that the SSL VPN you choose can implement such an access scheme. Verifying such capabilities is essential, as for an SSL VPN to deliver its full potential it must offer the ability to limit access within applications. Without such a capability, a 'lowest-common-denominator' approach (as discussed in Chapter 4) would need to be used to ensure security and would seriously and unnecessarily compromise the productivity of many users.

Also, it is important to note that sometimes an application that does not work via an SSL VPN at the application level can quickly be modified to make it work as such. This is especially true in the case of Flash-based menus, simple Java applications, and so on where replacing such code with code in an alternative language can often do the trick.

Proper User Interface and Experience

Although all SSL VPNs offer a graphical user interface, the nature of the interface varies dramatically between products. Several important items to take note of while considering SSL VPN solutions include:

- **Support for Access from Handheld Devices**: A growing number of remote users are accessing corporate resources from handheld devices such as those running PalmOS, PocketPC, or Symbian operating systems. Most SSL VPN vendors claim that their products will allow access from handheld devices. However, organizations considering deploying an SSL VPN should test how well each SSL VPN under consideration actually functions with any specific handheld devices it issues, as not all SSL VPNs work with all devices.

- **Flexibility of the GUI**: Built-in standard GUIs vary between SSL VPN products, and the criteria for selecting the ideal one for a particular group or organization varies across organizations. Assuming that an SSL VPN is being deployed to a general audience (and not just to a small group of technical folks), an optimal GUI is usually one that allows users to work with a relatively simple-to-use interface as soon as the SSL VPN is installed, but that also can be thoroughly customized.

The ability to modify the user interface is often a significant factor in user satisfaction levels. Users of all SSL VPN products use web browsers to achieve remote access. So some portions of the interface are fixed across products. Yet, despite the underlying uniformity, the actual interface that appears within browser windows differs tremendously between products, as does the level of flexibility and customizability provided to system administrators and users.

Most SSL VPNs allow basic elements of the GUI to be customized, for example, the color of the portal page background, a corporate logo to be loaded onto the page, creation of user bookmarks, etc. However, such basic modifications to a standard interface do not really allow organizations to modify the system to work the way their users want it to work.

If large numbers of users are to use the SSL VPN, then there will certainly be different interfaces required for different segments of the user population. Systems should always offer users the ability to work the way they are used to working in the office and not restrict them by means of an unfamiliar or inefficient interface.

Additionally, depending on how critical access from handheld devices is, it may be wise to verify that the SSL VPN can optimize the user interface for handheld devices with small screens.

- **Multiple language support**: Multi-language support is important in most multi-national corporations and other environments in which multiple languages are used in business. Several factors should be considered:

  o It may be useful to have the SSL VPN dynamically set the language used for the user interface of a particular session based on the configuration settings on the access device.

  o Organizations in non-English speaking countries may not need multi-language support—just local language support (i.e., all sessions are in some particular non-English language). Organizations conducting business in multiple countries will likely want their SSL VPN to be able to simultaneously support multiple languages.

  o If users will utilize non-Latin character sets such as Cyrillic, Hebrew, or Japanese, or data in non-Latin characters will be accessed via the SSL VPN, the SSL VPN should be tested to verify that it can support such access.

  o Of course, if a company conducts all of its business in an area that speaks only one language, multi-language functionality is extraneous and need not be tested.

- **Secure Single Sign On**: If your organization plans to leverage the Single-Sign-On capabilities offered by most SSL VPNs, it is important to verify that the SSO offered by the product is the SSO that you plan to use. Several SSO functionalities were described in previous chapters. Make sure that the SSL VPN offers the type that meets your business requirements and will integrate into your environment.

- **Existing Portal Integration**: If your organization has an existing portal, it may be (and usually is) advantageous to use each user's standard portal home page as his or her remote access home page. The user experience would be identical when remote and when in the office—reducing help-desk calls and the like.

Remote Password Management

For passwords to be an effective access-control mechanism they must be changed regularly; using the same password for a long period seriously increases the chances of it being compromised and misused.

SSL VPN access, however, presents some problems vis-à-vis password management. If an organization forces its users to change passwords every so often by expiring old passwords, users who are on the road when the expiration occurs will be locked out of their applications and files.

As such, organizations considering investing in an SSL VPN should seriously consider whether they want to offer remote password management. If they do, it is imperative to verify that the SSL VPN they want to deploy supports such a function.

An SSL VPN that offers remote password management should prompt remote users when passwords are about to expire and also enable people to update passwords using any web browser.

On a similar note, enterprises that plan to use two-factor authentication as an access control mechanism should ensure that the SSL VPN supports updates to their authentication system. For example, in the case of token-based authentication mechanisms that utilize a server stored-PIN (e.g., RSA SecurID), the SSL VPN should offer remote management for the PIN codes associated with tokens.

Adherence to Security Standards

All SSL VPNs offer security functionality, but security capabilities vary greatly between products. Proper planning demands that products be evaluated to determine how well they conform to your enterprise's particular security guidelines and policies. SSL VPN technology and security considerations have been discussed in detail earlier in this book, but several often overlooked items are highlighted below, as they are areas in which SSL

VPN technology often violates corporate security policies without the knowledge of the organization deploying it. Organizations reviewing SSL VPN products should be certain that they can answer the following questions:

- **Connection and accessibility**: Does the SSL VPN force you to establish a network-type connection from any non-corporate-owned computer to the internal network? Does it rely on network-type connections to make any critical applications work? If the organization blocks network-type connections will applications still be able to work remotely? What about port forwarding—which applications work if port forwarding is turned off?

- **Integration with IDS**: Does the SSL VPN integrate well with Intrusion Detection Systems (IDS)? Does it perform any actions that generate *false positive* alerts? Can it support host-based IDS on the SSL VPN server?

- **Firewall**: Does the SSL VPN allow protocols that are supposed to be blocked at the perimeter firewall to tunnel into the organization through encapsulation in an SSL tunnel? If so, where will they be blocked? Will a firewall need to be installed on the SSL VPN device?

- **Application firewalling**: Does the SSL VPN provide application firewalling that blocks all requests not known to be safe, or does it simply check for properly formatted HTML (in which case worms and hacker attacks may enter the corporate network and compromise internal systems)?

- **Timeouts and session termination**: Does the SSL VPN offer inactivity timeouts that work even if the user abandons the session with a page displayed in the browser window that incorporates auto-refresh requests? Are users warned before sessions are terminated?

- **Data Caching**: Does the SSL VPN wipe cached data from access devices in a secure fashion or does it simply *delete* it (in which case it is usually recoverable by unauthorized parties as described in Chapter 4)? Does it erase information that is stored in non-standard locations? If virtual storage areas are used, do all of the applications that need to be accessed remotely work with such storage areas?

- **Testing and Certification**: Has the SSL VPN been certified by any independent security auditors? Did they audit the security of using the product (including client-side issues) or simply the resilience of the appliance to specific type of attacks? Was the auditor an objective third party preparing a report on SSL VPNs or was he or she paid by a particular vendor to conduct the test? Was the product tested with a configuration similar to the one for which you plan to use it? Would implementing the product using the configuration in which it was tested enable you to meet your business needs?

Platform

Key items related to the SSL VPN platform that are often overlooked but of which note should be taken are highlighted below:

Hardware

Some SSL VPNs come as appliances, some as software that must be installed onto computers provided by the implementer, and others offer an option of selecting either of these form factors. There is no one *right* option—an appliance makes installation simpler, but some organizations may prefer to use a standard hardware supplier and server configuration to simplify management. In any event, make sure that the SSL VPN you choose offers a platform that you are comfortable in maintaining long term.

Operating System

As discussed in Chapter 4, various versions of Microsoft Windows and Linux are the most common operating environments for SSL VPN servers. In general, it is wise to select an SSL VPN that runs on an operating system with which your system administrators are already comfortable, and upon which any standard administration and management tools already in use throughout your organization can be used.

Network Connectivity

Today's SSL VPNs typically offer either 100BaseT or 1000BaseT (i.e., Gigabit Ethernet) connectivity. Reality, however, dictates that only a miniscule number of organizations have Internet connectivity that even approaches such speeds. As such, 100BaseT probably supports far more data throughput than the SSL VPN will ever need to handle. The bottleneck in an SSL VPN implementation is almost never the connection of the SSL VPN server to the network, and, as such, it is unlikely that the speed of the **Network Interface Card (NIC)** will affect SSL VPN performance.

One important exception to the above is that if the SSL VPN will be used internally (i.e., users on the internal network will access systems through the SSL VPN). In this case, higher bandwidth to the SSL VPN servers may help, although even this is questionable (as the NIC is likely to be much faster than other portions of the SSL VPN technology).

Determining which SSL VPN Functions to Use

SSL VPNs offer numerous features and functions, some of which may not be necessary (or even advisable) to use for particular implementations. The decision as to which SSL VPN capabilities an organization should utilize is directly tied to its business aims. Some common scenarios are described earlier in this chapter. In addition, some important items to note as basic guidelines include:

1. Application-level access should be used for general access. When applications offer a web interface, the web interface should be offered via the SSL VPN.

2. It is inefficient and undesirable to use terminal-services-type access for accessing applications with web interfaces. Doing so hurts the performance and unnecessarily limits the number of points from which the applications can be accessed.

3. Network tunneling may be used for power users from trusted devices, but should not be offered when accessing from machines not known to be secure. Port forwarding, etc. should also only be used with caution in such scenarios.

4. Whenever Telnet is allowed, it should be allowed only with per-user, per-resource, per-source, and per-destination limitations (e.g., Joe can use Telnet from his laptop to server 1.2.3.4).

5. Network tunneling and port forwarding should never be used as "band-aid"—that is to make applications work that should be delivered at the application level but for some reason do not work at the application level with a particular SSL VPN product (e.g., sophisticated web applications used for customer access).

6. Cache cleaning should be done on all machines other than trusted machines.

7. Timeout thresholds can be set much higher on trusted machines than untrusted.

Where to Deploy the SSL VPN server

As discussed in Chapter 4, proper deployment of an SSL VPN server within enterprise infrastructure is critical for ensuring a secure implementation.

We will now examine the pros and cons of locating the SSL VPN server in various locations within a typical organization's infrastructure. (None of these architectures is perfect; it is important for people considering deploying an SSL VPN to understand the ramifications of using each architecture before deciding on which one to choose.)

Back Office

One option is to place the SSL VPN onto an internal network as shown below:

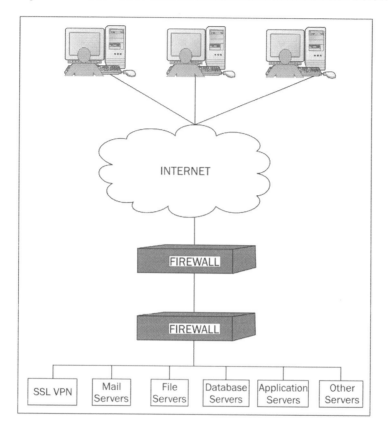

Pros

Locating an SSL VPN on an internal network offers the following benefits over alternative architectures:

- No ports other than the one for SSL (and maybe also for regular HTTP so users who do not type HTTPS can be redirected) need to be opened in any perimeter firewalls
- Decryption of SSL-encrypted traffic is performed in the secure back office
- SSL keys are stored on a secure network where they are protected from being compromised

Cons

As discussed in Chapter 4, placing the SSL VPN server on the internal network may create several problems:

- **Undermines firewall infrastructure**: It may undermine the entire firewall infrastructure. Protocols that firewalls are supposed to block are tunneled using SSL all the way to the internal network. By the time the SSL VPN server reconstitutes the native communication formats, the contents of those communications are already on the internal network where they certainly do not belong.

- **Network-based IDSs on DMZ rendered ineffective**: Any network-based IDSs present on the DMZ will be rendered ineffective. IDSs work by scanning network packets as they traverse a network—placing IDSs on a DMZ is a good technique for stopping rogue traffic from entering a corporate network. However, in the case of an SSL VPN on the internal network, all requests are encrypted with SSL. If the requests traverse the DMZ in an encrypted form, the IDSs will not be able to read them. IDSs will probably be unable to distinguish between valid user activity and even the most severe of attacks.

- **Unfettered access to the internal network**: If the SSL VPN server is compromised by a hacker or worm, the mischievous party would have unfettered and unrestricted access to the internal network to which the SSL VPN server is connected.

- **Remote node could serve as a bridge to another network**: It is possible that the remote node could serve as a bridge to another network as described earlier. If a remote user is allowed to establish a network-type connection over SSL, it is possible that anyone on that user's local network will be able to connect to the internal network via the access device used to access the SSL VPN. This poses a threat to an organization's corporate infrastructure.

- **Unauthenticated parties are able to send network packets to internal network**: Allowing such access violates standard corporate security policies, and, for good reason. Hackers and worms should not have *any* level of access to corporate resources. Offering them such access can lead to **Denial of Service (DoS)** attacks, mapping of the corporate network, scanning for vulnerabilities that can be leveraged to pilfer data or commandeer control over computers, etc.

DMZ

Placing an SSL VPN server in a DMZ is a common scenario as shown below:

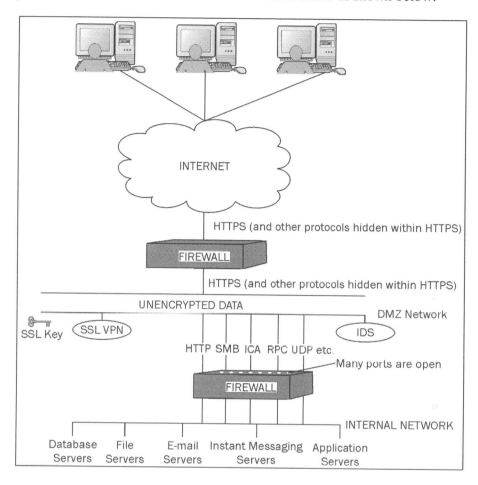

Pros

This scenario was also mentioned in Chapter 4. It offers several benefits over locating an SSL VPN server in the back office:

- Unwanted protocols may be blocked by the interior firewall.
- Only trusted parties are granted access to internal resources; all untrusted parties are stopped in the DMZ.
- Network-based IDS can work on both the DMZ and internal networks.
- Using a DMZ offers a layered approach to security.

Cons

Locating an SSL VPN server in a DMZ poses several problems (alluded to in Chapter 4):

- **SSL decryption keys maintained in an unsafe environment**: If SSL keys are compromised, attackers may be able to impersonate the organization. Criminals who utilize phishing to steal sensitive information from users would love to obtain corporate SSL keys. Placing such keys in an untrusted or semi-trusted location is not wise.

- **Decryption performed in an insecure area**: So, communication of sensitive information occurs as plaintext (not encrypted) on the insecure DMZ network where it may be subject to sniffing and pilfering. As such, the SSL VPN is not affording true end-to-end encryption—it is delivering end-to-middle encryption, as the contents of the SSL session are decrypted in an insecure location outside of the destination network.

- **SSL VPN undermines exterior firewall**: If a remote user is allowed to establish network connectivity over SSL, the user can essentially transmit any protocol by embedding network packets within HTTPS. This means that protocols that are supposed to be blocked by the exterior firewall slip by as they are tunneled within HTTPS to the DMZ. When administrators configure the exterior firewall to block a specific port so as to disable use of a particular service from the Internet, they want that service blocked. Allowing communications to circumvent such security barriers is a serious problem and likely violates organizational security policies. (Note that in the case of IPSec VPN the same device that acts as the firewall terminates the VPN connection; this is typically not the case with SSL VPN.)

- **Numerous ports need to be opened in the interior firewall**: This would enable inappropriate types of communications between the DMZ and the internal network. Opening such ports compromises the effectiveness of the interior firewall, blends the DMZ and Internet environments, and introduces serious security concerns. Additionally, opening such ports typically violates corporate security guidelines.

- **Remote node could serve as a bridge to another network**: As described earlier, if a remote user is allowed to establish a network-type connection over SSL it is possible that anyone on that user's local network will be able to connect to the internal network via the device used to access SSL VPN.

- **External parties might become nodes on organizational networks**. Most security-conscious organizations prohibit any computer not belonging to the organization from becoming a node on the organization's network. If an SSL VPN is used for partners, customers, and prospects to access corporate resources, and if the SSL VPN allows remote users to establish network connectivity over SSL, then this policy will be violated (and the risks that the policy seeks to mitigate will pose a serious threat).

- **Access to attack internal servers**: If a hacker or worm compromises the SSL VPN server, the mischievous party will have access to a machine from which he/she/it can launch attacks against internal servers.

Outside the Perimeter Firewall

Another possible location for an SSL VPN is outside the perimeter firewall

Pros

The benefits of placing an SSL VPN outside the perimeter firewall include:

- Unwanted protocols do not enter the organization—not even into the DMZ.
- Untrusted parties cannot enter an organization's DMZ or its internal network.
- Network-based Intrusion Detection Systems can work on both the DMZ and internal networks.

Cons

There are several serious problems with such an implementation including:

- **SSL VPN has no protection against network-level attacks**: Unless the SSL VPN itself contains a full network-level firewall, by placing it in an unprotected environment you are asking for serious trouble. The magnitude of this problem generally disqualifies the entire option of placing an SSL VPN outside the perimeter firewall.

- **SSL decryption keys are maintained in an extremely unsafe environment**: As discussed above regarding DMZs, in the current scenario the keys are stored in an even worse location—on the public Internet. If SSL decryption is offloaded to a server or appliance on a more interior network (to avoid storing keys on an unsafe network) then communication paths must be established between the Internet (i.e., outside the exterior firewall) and internal servers, which also poses serious security concerns.

- **Numerous ports may need to be opened in the firewall/s**: This would enable inappropriate types of communications between the Internet and the internal networks. Opening such ports typically violates corporate security guidelines and undermines the purpose of having firewalls in the first place.

The implementation is as shown in the following figure:

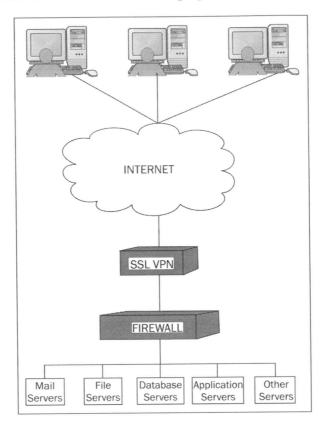

Air Gap

Air Gap and similar technologies help address some of the concerns of the previous architectures. Air Gap entails using two servers to service SSL VPN requests, one connected to the internal network and one to a DMZ. The external server receives user requests, while the internal server performs all SSL VPN processing and security functions. In between the two computers, there is no network connection, but rather a memory bank that is shared between them, which (at least in some implementations) can only be accessed by one of the servers at any point in time. As shown overleaf, an Air Gap switch regulates which computer can access the memory bank at any moment:

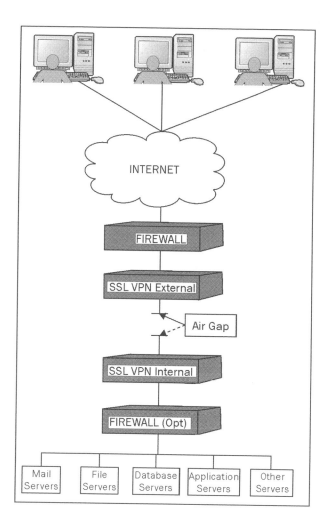

Pros

Air Gap technology maintains a disconnection between the Internet and internal servers, and offers improvements upon the standard DMZ-deployment model discussed above.

- It ensures that any machine that can be reached at a network level by untrusted users does not have access to the internal network. Even if the SSL VPN external server is compromised by hackers and/or worms, such parties will not be able to connect to internal systems.
- The SSL VPN is much harder to compromise as operating system vulnerabilities cannot be exploited on the internal server.

- SSL decryption keys are maintained on the safe internal network or on a more secure DMZ without having to open communications ports for SSL-decryption related communications.
- Ports are not opened in firewalls network-connected to the Internet.

Cons

The major drawback of Air Gap technology is that it typically costs more to implement than simpler architectures. As alluded to earlier, as a result, Air Gap may be ideal for security-conscious medium or large size firms, but is often overkill for small companies.

Offloaded SSL

Offloading SSL to an SSL processor on the same network can make sense. The image below shows an example of offloading SSL processing from outside the perimeter firewall to the DMZ:

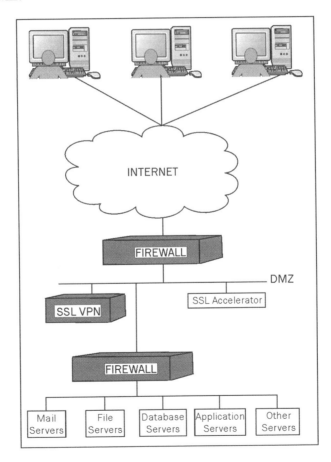

However, the use of an offloaded SSL accelerator can also impact architecture. For example, offloading SSL decryption from a less secure network to a more internal SSL processor can produce various effects. Examples of this scenario include:

- Offloading SSL processing from outside the perimeter firewall to the DMZ
- Offloading SSL processing from the DMZ to the back office
- Offloading SSL processing from an exterior DMZ to an interior DMZ

In all these cases, there are similar pros and cons.

The following image shows offloading of SSL processing from the DMZ to back office:

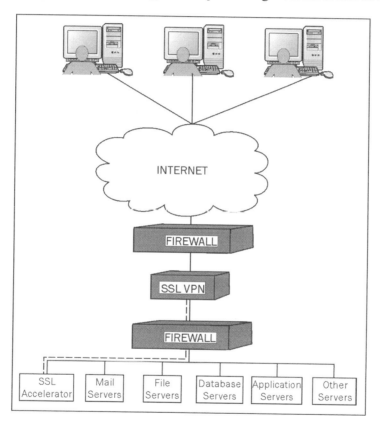

Pros

Decryption takes place in a more secure environment than it would without such offloading. SSL keys are stored in a safer environment than they would be without such offloading

Cons

There is, however, a serious drawback. For communications to occur between the SSL VPN server on the less secure network and the accelerator in the more secure environment, communications ports must be opened—meaning that the layered security strategy is weakened.

Planning for Deployment

Although no generic task list can serve as a true checklist to be used for preparing to implement an SSL VPN, the following is a list of several items that demand consideration during design stages, but which can be easily overlooked:

- **Externally accessible IP addresses—one per SSL VPN portal**: Security technologies such as Network Address Translation may allow an internal IP number to be used. Also, if Air Gap technology is used, the implementation may require an appropriate IP number for each server. If multiple SSL VPN servers will be used in conjunction with a load balancer then the single Internet-accessible virtual IP number will need to be known as will the real IP numbers of the SSL VPN servers.

- **Externally accessible DNS name—one per SSL VPN portal**: If a load balancer is being used then the externally accessible DNS name for accessing the SSL VPN will need to be known, as well as any DNS names of the real SSL VPN servers (the latter may not be needed if those servers are always referred to by IP addresses).

- **IP addresses and DNS names of internal systems**: You will need to know the IP addresses and DNS names of any internal systems to which you want to provide remote access. If the SSL VPN you are using does not have application modules that automatically configure ports etc. for each application you are planning to publish to remote users, you will likely also need to know the ports used for communications by the various applications.

- **Accessible authentication and user-directory systems**: Access to any authentication and user-directory systems with which the SSL VPN will interface will be needed.

- **External SSL accelerator IP number**: The IP number for any external SSL accelerator that will be used by the SSL VPN to improve reliability or performance should be known. If an SSL accelerator is installed into the SSL VPN server, instructions as to how to integrate it should be known.

- **Security policies**: This includes all of the policies that govern access.

- **Physical accommodations**: These include:

o   Rack space in the computer-room or the data center where the equipment will be housed

o   Network cabling

o   Power cables

o   Uninterruptible Power Supplies (UPS)

User and Administrator Training

Proper training of both users and administrators is critical to any successful technology implementation. Despite its leveraging common web browsers as the primary user software, SSL VPN is not an exception. Users must be made to feel comfortable with their remote-access system, and, although far less training is usually necessary than with earlier remote-access technologies, attention must be given to preparing users for the adoption of or transition to SSL remote access. As such, the topic of training will not be discussed as simply a part of the preparation for implementing an SSL VPN, but rather, as an entire chapter: Chapter 6.

Summary

In this chapter we discussed how to plan for an SSL VPN implementation. We covered:

- Determining business requirements
- How to select an appropriate SSL VPN product—including a discussion of several factors that are often overlooked but may affect the success and long-term viability of an SSL VPN implementation

In the next chapter we will discuss educating users about SSL VPN.

6

Educating the User

SSL VPNs provide a mechanism to communicate securely between two points with an insecure network in between them. Yet, there is no technology on the planet that will totally protect computing operations on its own. End users need to be security-conscious if the security technology is to do its job.

Think about your own organization. Can someone call a user on the phone, profess that he or she is from the 'help desk' and ask for a username and password? In most cases, such a call will not happen, but if it was made, would anyone in your organization actually give their credentials to the caller? If they did, the entire expensive authentication infrastructure you have in place would be undermined.

A combination of solid technology *and* an educated end user is necessary for security. We have already covered the technology used to secure SSL VPNs; now we address end-user training.

The next section discusses formal training plans; people from organizations that already have such systems in place may want to skip to the *Specific Training for SSL VPNs* section later in this chapter.

Building an Education Plan

Whether the user is a customer, a new hire, or a long-term employee, training is essential. The user must feel confident in the system in place and must feel encouraged to use it. They must know that SSL VPN is there to help them in their work and that it is safe to use. They must also take an active part in enabling it to work smoothly and safely. A feeling of ownership needs to be created; the user needs to feel part of the solution. In order to involve the end users in your security system you will need to create an education and training plan. This plan should identify the details of each activity needed to accommodate your education goals. The plan should include the following:

- A training charter (or reference to any corporate charters)
- Education goals

- The development needs of any training
- The delivery process for any training
- Systems, tools, and materials
- Metrics that will be used to identify how successful the training is
- The roles and responsibilities for the training
- The implementation (or schedules) of any training

The training can involve a workshop, using Computer Based Training (CBT), Web-Based Training (WBT), or even classroom training. The company must make a decision on what type of education and training is needed.

You will need to understand the demographics of your user base. If most of your users are customers, then you will not be able to get them to attend any formal training classes. This decision is dependent on many variables such as the number of employees involved, or the location and type of customer.

A workshop type of approach may be best when introducing SSL VPN if it is new to the users and they have no prior experience with it. Later the training of new hires or retraining of employees already familiar with this type of Internet access could be accomplished by CBTs, WBTs, or possibly distance learning.

Education Plan: Start the Process

We begin by starting the process of building an education plan.

> The process described here is formal and structured. Real-life training plans may follow this example or may be simpler; the information below is intended strictly as a guideline.

The following flowchart gives a graphical representation of the different steps involved in building an education plan:

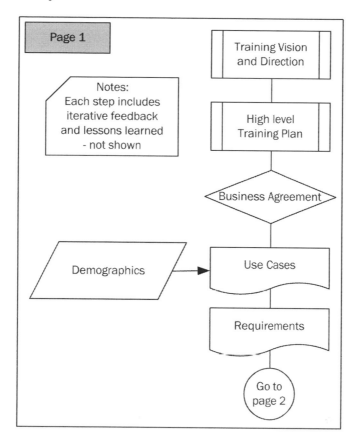

Vision

First off, you need to have the vision of what you want your end-users to know about security. The goals of your education plan need to be defined. Once you have identified your vision you need to create a basic plan to communicate it (as part of this process will include executive and management buy-in).

High-Level Training Plan

The high-level training plan is just that—high level. This will be the executive summary that details the vision, goals, and ultimately the implementation of your plan. It will contain the expected long-term benefits of educating the end user on security issues.

The Agreement

Following down on the flowchart, you will see *business agreement.* If you are in a small company, then you may make the decision and go forward. Larger companies may have a board that you will need to present your vision and plan to. At some point, you will need some type of approval to go forward.

The Use Case

The use case (or use case scenario) is a tool that you can use to describe the basic (functional) requirements of each education or training need. This, combined with a demographic analysis, will help you specify how users in specific roles will use the system. Inputs into the user case are business needs, demographics, systemic dependencies, and technology.

Education Plan: Finalize the Plan

The next step is to finalize the plan.

Final Training Plan

This is the detailed plan that will go before any approval boards. The following elements should be included:

- Requirements from the previous steps
- Copy of each use case
- Budget estimates and justification
- Decision records from each line of business (if needed)

The flowchart below shows the details to be considered while finalizing the plan:

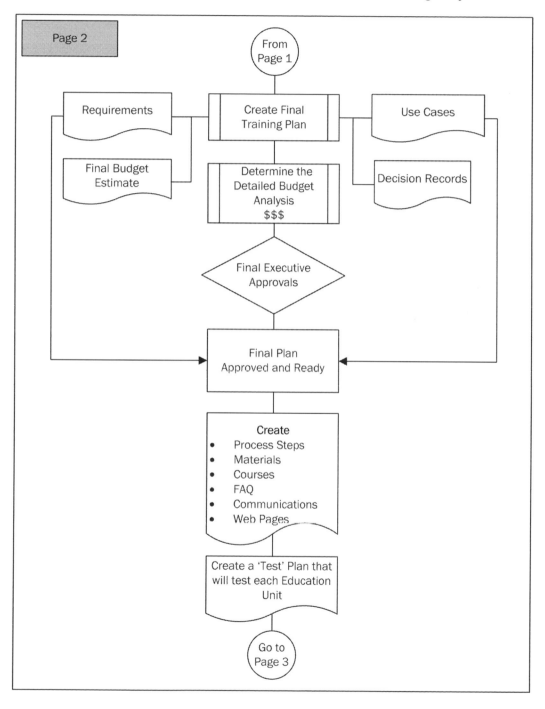

Include Incident Handling Policies in your Training Plan

Levels of response urgency need to be defined. An incident response team is an important part of any holistic security plan and should comprise of representatives from:

- Management
- Legal Counsel
- Technical Personnel
- Team Coordinators
- Communication Specialists

The basic procedures for handling an incident need to be defined. If an incident occurs, each of the following points must be implemented:

- **Preparation**: The team must have a charter in place
- **Incident Detection**: Tools and processes must be in place in order to detect an incident
- **Immediate Action Plan**: Needs to be prioritized based on the level of importance
- **Communications**: This is critical for handling an incident. Plan ahead how you will communicate to end users about any issues and systemic incidents
- **Detailed Situation Analysis**: Make observations and record what happened
- **Recovery**: Try to recover any erased data
- **Feedback**: How can we prevent this from happening again?

End users will need to know and understand their part in addressing security incidents. Be sure to include these procedures in your overall education plan.

The Money

When all is said and done, it will come down to cash. The executive will ask: "How much?" Make sure you have good estimates; it is normally difficult to get more money once the training has begun. All companies operate under budget constraints.

Creating Educational Materials

As shown on page 2 of the flow chart, it is time to create the education materials needed. Since updates to security will be occurring as risks to the Internet change, the materials used need to be flexible enough to allow for changes to content as needed. Some of the types of materials that need to be created are actual courses, books, FAQs, web pages, and system communication.

Reusing the Use Cases

If you did a good job of creating the use cases, you will be able to use each scenario as a test case. Build a test plan that will test each element of your education. This test should include reading course materials, testing the courses, and reviewing the communications.

Executing the Test Plan

We are now headed down the final stretch; the next diagram will lead you through a series of pilots. The test plan has been created, now it is time to execute the test plan.

Education Plan: Testing and Pilots

This diagram takes you through the execution of a test plan:

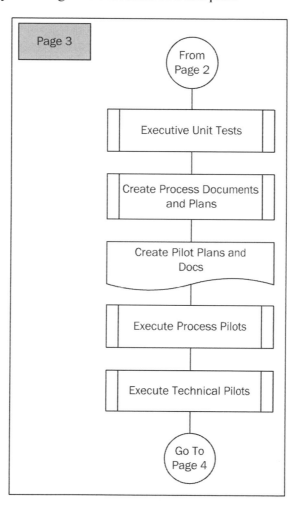

Unit Tests

Unit tests will include the testing of individual components of the education materials and courses. One example would be Web-Based Training. One of the elements would be to make sure that the web server is running and the base software is loaded and working.

Process Tests

This is where you will need to test the process of delivering the education; one example would be a tracking system to monitor the status of each person as he or she has been trained. Also, does the delivery of the education require more than one person? If so, then you will need to make sure that each person knows his or her part of this process.

Technical Pilots

It is time to bring all of the technical components together. This is where you will test all components holistically—the on-line courses, the tracking system, and communication. All technical components will be tested in this stage. So far in your education plan you have tested all of the technical components, both unit and holistic. Then you tested the delivery process. Now it is time to test it for real.

Production Pilot 1

This is your first run with real users. If possible, make this a small group. Run the whole process from step 1 to the last step and be sure to document each success and issue. Then review the pilots for lessons learned. Use the lessons learned in the next pilot. Also, if possible never put an executive into pilot group 1.

Production Pilot 2

This group should be as large as a normal training session. Now you are running as near *real* mode as possible. Once again, review the lessons learned, and prepare to roll out the training to the enterprise.

Implementation

This is the moment of truth, and you are ready to go. All tests are done, and the end users are ready. Time to roll out the training to the enterprise; if you have followed the steps above then you will be ready.

Education Plan: Production

The following flow chart depicts the final review process:

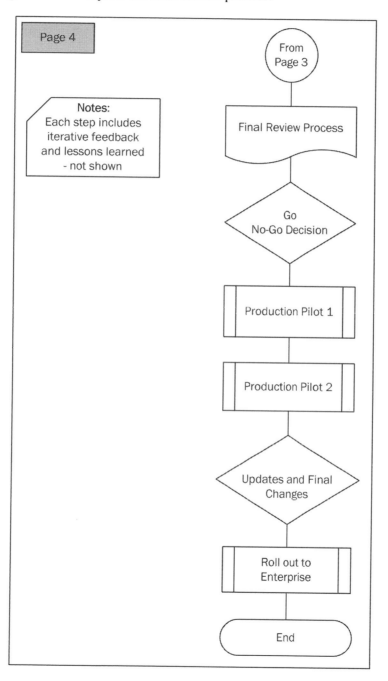

Review Process

Remember that you have been working on this plan iteratively, and you will be making changes to the plan, process, and technology as you go—all following your requirements, needs, and your use cases. If all is ready then you schedule production pilots.

Specific Training for SSL VPNs

It is true that SSL VPNs are generally user friendly; in many cases, direct end user training may not be needed if users have already been presented with general IT Security concepts during the general security awareness training. But you will still need to train your staff on support and maintenance of the SSL VPN. Also, you will still need to communicate with your customers and/or end users about how to access the system and who to call if they have problems. If the customer does call, who will answer the phone— your trained help desk. Understand your demographics.

Training the Masses

As mentioned, most SSL VPNs are easy to use. Most users that have any type of browser experience should be able to establish a session; just point to the URL and click. But there are some issues that should be mentioned to your end users and included in your training plan.

How to use an SSL VPN

User should be given information as to what is available for access via the SSL VPN as well as what client restrictions exist (for example, if you access from a machine without anti-virus, you will not be allowed to upload files). If users can configure bookmarks they should be taught how to do so. Of course, users should be instructed to log out when they complete sessions and should be taught about any timeout mechanisms in place. Users should also be told explicitly for what purposes they may not use the SSL VPN and what systems/data should not be accessed from public locations.

Social Engineering

This is also known as the non-technical hack. One simple example is a person calling you and saying, "I am from the bank, and I need to check your on-line account, can you verify your username and password with me?" Unbelievably, there are people who will give out their username and password over the phone to a stranger. Yes, users should be trained (reminded) about this risk. SSL VPNs are gateways into many systems—make sure your users guard their keys to the gate.

Phishing

Phishing attacks use spoofed e-mails and fake websites designed to fool recipients into providing personal financial data such as account usernames and passwords, credit card numbers, social security numbers, etc. A common technique is to use the names from well-known and trusted brands. Examples include known retailers, credit card companies, and banks. Eventually phishers may spoof SSL VPN access portals; users should know how to spot a 'phish'. Statistics related to phishing-type attacks can be found at the **Anti-Phishing Working Group** (**APWG**) website: http://www.antiphishing.org/.

Sharing Credentials

Users should be taught that their credentials (username, password, and PIN) should never be shared. Also putting the password under the keyboard is a bad idea. Users should be taught to protect and never to share one-time authentication tokens and other authentication devices.

Single Sign On (SSO)

Single Sign On is the ability to log on to a set of systems and services by logging on only once. SSO can use any number of credential factors, including:

- Username and password
- Tokens
- Smart cards
- USB authentications devices
- Public-Key Infrastructure (PKI)-based authentication

End users will need training on SSO and the possible security issues. One in particular is that a Single Sign On can provide a single source of access for hackers. So it will be very important for end-users to understand the following:

- Credential management
- Sharing of credentials
- Clearing sessions and logging out
- Help Desk support systems
- The process for using the SSO
- How to get credentials re-set
- What to do if a physical tokens or USB device is lost

As always, users should be trained to select a good password, which is difficult to guess and/or crack.

SSL Locks and Dialog Boxes: One More Note about Phishing

Many users have learned that the *lock* on their browser is a good thing, and the authors agree. The authors will also say this—not all locks are good. This may be a scary epiphany to many of you; but it is time to see the light.

HTTPS connections to servers will provide a lock once the one-way credentials have been established. This normally happens when a trusted **Certificate Authority (CA)** root certification has determined that the target server has the same ancestral root certificate. The only way that the server will get one of the certificates is that the server is *certified* with the CA's root certifier. Many CAs are considered trusted, because they have followed a set of rules as specified in a **Certification Practice Statement (CPS)**.

A CPS document will detail how the CAs have controlled their certifier. In the case of a company like Verisign, they have documented how they have controlled their certifier. In addition, they have provided browser-based certifies to browser manufactures—like Netscape and Microsoft.

The following screenshot shows an example of trusted certificate as certified by a third party public CA:

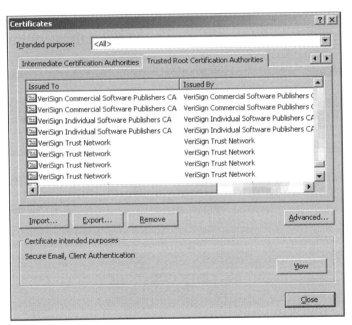

Hacker Patterns

A good analysis of hacker patterns can be found in the *Offensive Operations Model* whitepaper at http://www.penetrationtest.com/.

E-Commerce Scenario

You are the owner of an e-business called 'The Real Site', with the URL `http://www.therealsite.xyz/`. Back in March, you decided to accept credit cards and purchased a credit card processing application. As part of the requirements, you enabled SSL on your web server. You contacted a third-party certificate authority, like Verisign, and sent them a *safe copy* of your SSL key-ring file. The CA certified your server and sent you back your 'safe copy' with the certificate. You then merged the certified safe copy into your server and now you were able to run SSL.

The result of this action is that when an Internet Explorer (IE) browser connects to your site, it will then exchange certificates, and if the root keys match the end user, it will be allowed access—and then the user will see the famous lock at the bottom of the browser.

> **Server Key-ring File**
>
> The key-ring file holds the certified server certificate and the certificate authority root keys.

Phishing and the SSL Lock

Hacker Bob has decided to go Phishing, and he knows that people have been told to look for the lock. No problem for Bob, he knows that his target group has not been trained on browser warning messages. Therefore, he sends out the following message:

> Hello User at the RealSite.xyz:
>
> As part of an on-going security audit, we are asking our customers to check your Username, Password, and Secret code. Please enter the following URL below to access your account.
>
> Just click this URL: `https://therealsite.xyz/`
>
> Thanks for your help to keep your account updated.
>
> Signed
>
> Mr. CEO in Charge
>
> CEO The Real Site

At first glance, you look at the message above and you say, "Looks OK to me". If you look under the covers, at the page source, you will see the following code:

```
<br>
<a href="https://192.168.136.128"> https://therealsite.xyz</a><br>
<br>
```

You will notice that `https://therealsite.xyz/` is really linked to `192.168.136.128`. Once the end user clicks on this address, they will be sent to that address and not `therealsite.xyz`. This will catch many users, but the next screen may stop a few. The screenshot below shows that the root certificate in the browser does not match that of the server. This is a very important message: The server that is being accessed is not trusted by this browser. This is a great message if you know how to read it. The sad news is that there are too many words in this message. Sounds like a joke; it is not. Many users will just read the message and see the following:

The Top Bar—Security Alert and Do you want to proceed? Yes/No

Many users will hit Yes, and then they will be connected to the *secure* site.

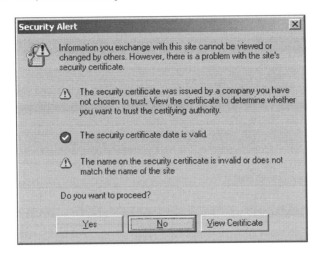

Yes, this site is network secure; it is running SSL on a generic certificate; a trusted third party CA (like Verisign) did not sign it. A self-signing certificate signed the certificate. Most end users will not understand this concept; as a result, they will just press Yes.

Once the end users press Yes, they will be presented with a screen that looks like The Real Site—or their bank, or some other institution that holds their private information. The end users will also see the lock as shown below:

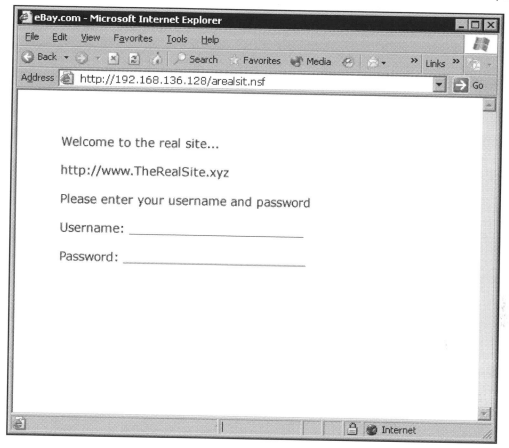

Very few will notice that they have connected to the wrong site. At this point, Hacker Bob will then harvest the information he was after.

Summary

We have reviewed the importance of end user education and the importance of a solid education plan. A framework for developing education plans in general was covered, as were some specific items that should be included for SSL VPN users.

In the next chapter SSL VPN access to legacy systems will be discussed.

7

Legacy Data Access

A computer, according to Webster's dictionary, is a machine or person that may be designed to carry out complex and lengthy mathematical analytical operations very rapidly, to control industrial operations, or to undertake clerical work. According to this definition, everyone who works for a government is, in essence, himself/herself a computer. So are the clerks who check you out at your local grocery store!

Keeping this in mind, it is easy to see that the true genealogical history of computing can be traced back to the formation of math as a tool in humankind's daily life. The first milestone of computing history might be regarded as the invention of the **Abacus**. Having emerged about 5,000 years ago in China, the abacus is still in use today.

Having a simple but reliable system of performing basic mathematical operations, this device was used for daily commerce by thousands of people throughout the Far East and, eventually, Asia Minor as well. Users were able to make computations utilizing a system of sliding beads arranged on a wooden rack, allowing early merchants to keep a track of trading transactions, in ways they had never been able to before. From those early roots, humankind was eventually able to manifest greater power in the computers of today.

This new age of computing began in the 1950s when John Backus and IBM developed the **FORTRAN** computer programming language. This first modern programming software provided mechanisms and tools to develop business applications. The next step came with the development of the **ARPANET**.

ARPANET, essentially an early and simpler version of the modern Internet, provided a mechanism for computers to communicate with each other through a set of interconnecting networks.

At about the same time computer commerce communication protocols were introduced. One in particular was **Electronic Data Interchange (EDI)**. The standard that emerged from this protocol was developed in the 1980s and was known as **ANSI X12**. This brings us to the present day.

With more than 800 million users, the Web has mutated into a multitude of tools for business and personal use. The abacus, though a long way from the Internet, was still both hardware and software, requiring an end user to operate the system. The Internet is not dissimilar in that, it comprises hardware, software, and end users.

ANSI X12

This comprises standards defining the structure, format, and content of business transactions conducted through Electronic Data Interchange. ANSI X12 was produced by the committee ASC X12, supported by the **Data Interchange Standards Association, Inc. (DISA)**.

Computing Elements

Modern computers operate in much the same way as the abacus. Most computing services use the following elements to provide a complete computing experience:

- Hardware
- Operating system software
- Networks
- End users
- Applications (business, games, and databases)

Applications

A computer application is a program or group of programs designed to provide a particular solution to business requirements, end user needs, and/or technical requirements. End user applications can run as standalone applications and/or via a network. Let us analyze one example: you decide to purchase another copy of this book from an on-line store. The application involved could include:

- Firmware included in your computer
- Your computer's operating system
- Your web browser
- The Internet (defined as a collection of networks)
- The target web servers that receive your request
- Server operating systems
- Middleware software that connects to the transaction services
- The transaction software

- Databases
- Directories
- Support software (backup, disaster recovery, monitoring, and reporting)
- Shipping applications

As you can see, there are many different systems involved with network-based computing. These systems can translate into several different languages, and can cross the world. There are thousands of applications for **Personal Computers (PCs)**, mainframes, and web servers. The business world works from applications: these can be EDI-based, personal accounting programs, and web e-commerce systems.

Commercial Off-The-Shelf (COTS)

Many applications are known as **Commercial Off-The-Shelf (COTS)** programs. This is where you purchase a pre-built program, make a few configuration changes, and then begin using your application.

Other application types include millions of **custom** programs. These systems offer a unique flexibility that COTS programs cannot match. These applications are created to meet specific business needs and many can be created very quickly. The downside of COTS programs is that many of them are not created based on any standards, and have no formal support systems.

As e-commerce started to emerge, both COTS programs and custom programs started to move into web-based services. Many COTS programs started to provide direct web and HTTP services as part of their core programming.

Custom Programs

Custom programs were a bit slower to jump into the web world. Even today, many custom programs do not have direct web interfaces, and there are still custom programs that require specialized clients and server software. The world of the ubiquitous web interface with access to *any* application has not manifested itself…yet.

Legacy Applications

In the context of web access, those applications that do not provide a web-based interface are known as **legacy applications**. In information technology, legacy applications and data are those that have been inherited from languages, platforms, and techniques earlier than the current technology. Most enterprises using computers have legacy applications and databases that serve critical business needs. Typically, the challenge is to keep the legacy application running while converting it to newer, more efficient code that makes use of new technology and programmer skills.

Overall, legacy applications are those that comprise languages, techniques, and platforms that are not based on newer technologies. At this point you may ask, "OK, so should we just upgrade our computers to the newest models and install the latest web-enabled software?" Many of these programs are very expensive, and it can take years to convert some programs into direct web-based programs. In addition, the mentality in many companies is, "if it isn't broken, don't fix it." So you will find many of these legacy applications that will be running for many years to come.

The biggest change for many legacy applications occurred when most enterprise companies updated code to incorporate the year 2000 (Y2K) fix. Some applications were re-written to accommodate newer technology, and some were just 'fixed' in place. Even today there are still many old 'Y2K-fixed' applications running.

The Web Challenge

Many companies have a business need to access legacy applications securely from remote locations. SSL VPN seems ideal as the remote access technology with the lowest total cost of ownership. But how exactly does SSL VPN technology provide access to legacy applications?

SSL VPN solves this challenge by using the following two methods: **direct access** and **middleware access**.

Direct Access

SSL VPNs can provide direct access to a large variety of applications. Direct access via an SSL VPN may eliminate the need for server-based 'middleware' and other types of remote access systems and associated remote-access clients. Direct SSL VPN access into a trusted network, as shown in the following diagram, provides connectivity to many Web-based intranet applications.

SSL VPN direct access can also provide connectivity to non Web-enabled legacy applications. These applications can exist on AS/400, Windows, Unix/Linux systems, and other types of platforms. Some SSL VPN appliances connect to legacy-type applications by providing clientless remote access to legacy applications through the incorporation of web-enabling technology directly within the platform. Several such technologies were described in Chapter 3. The advantage of this approach is that end users need only a browser to access these remotely hosted applications.

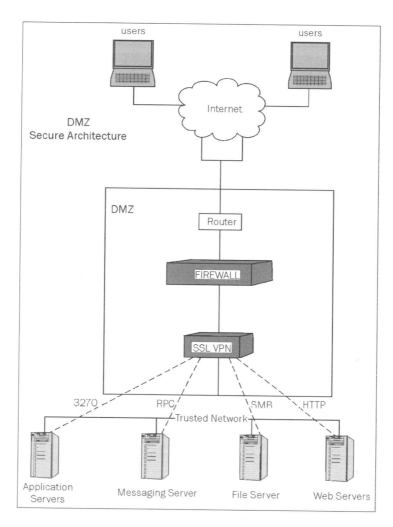

Scrape the Screen

Legacy application SSL VPN-based access can use built-in **screen-scraping tools**. These tools will split the emulation and display processing so that only the application's display is sent to the user's web browser. These tools are implemented either via a downloaded browser enhancement (usually an applet) or by calling special software previously installed on an access device.

Awareness

Another method of providing access is one in which an SSL VPN vendor provides an application-awareness engine. This engine will understand the architecture and dynamics of the systems to which it is providing access and handles the webification accordingly. This method provides a more seamless connection into legacy applications.

SSL VPN with Middleware Access

SSL VPNs, along with middleware, can provide a great range of legacy application access. Many companies are creating middleware-based portals. These portals provide a singular access point into both current-standard-based and legacy-based applications. The following diagram illustrates this technique for accessing legacy applications:

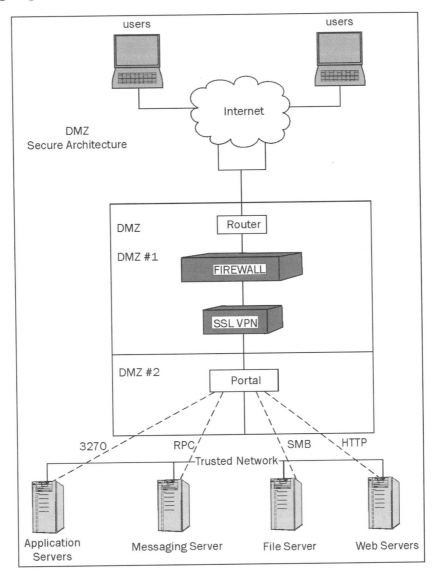

Legacy applications can be accessed though a set of portal connectors, also known as **portlets**. Some portlets provide legacy-based connectors, like a 3270 emulator connector.

Others can provide **Remote Procedural Calls (RPC)** access, transaction processing, messaging access, and Web access. One example of a web-based portlet is one using web services. **Web Services Architecture (WSA)** is a set of technologies that can provide web-based access to enterprise legacy applications. Web service technologies can also provide services that can hide some of the complexity of the legacy application interface.

The middleware serves as a buffer between the SSL VPN and the legacy application and handles all the transformations necessary to make the legacy applications ready for the SSL VPN server to publish remotely. Of course, the SSL VPN may still need to convert internal references and perform other remote-access related conversions.

Meeting the Challenge

As you can see, by using direct access and/or access with a portal, an SSL VPN appliance makes client/server applications available to remote users through the Web. SSL VPNs provide companies the flexibility to access their existing legacy application infrastructure without costly application re-development. SSL VPN access techniques can provide access to almost any application on any platform.

Secure Access

Most SSL VPN devices extend these legacy resources to authorized users. This process is implemented by the use of browser-based access to web-based resources using HTTP reverse-proxy technology. A single point of entry via the SSL VPN gateway provides a unified secure access point into a trusted legacy environment. In many cases, the SSL VPN can provide the authentication process, while still leaving the authorization process to the legacy application.

Tunneling to the Other Side

Another option for legacy access is by SSL VPN tunneling. The remote access methods described above meet the access needs of most remote users. Some users, however, may require client/server application access. In this case, a local client is installed on the user's PC and a remote server provides the services. Examples include CRM, e-mail, and custom applications. This can be provided by means of SSL tunneling technology as described in Chapter 3.

Tunneling Techniques

One example of this tunneling is implemented by the SSL VPN device using a built-in screen-scraping protocol that splits the emulation and display processing so that only the application's display is sent to the remote user's web browser.

In another technique, the SSL VPN will enable a small Java applet to download to the user's browser. The user will connect to the SSL VPN via a browser and authenticate. The applet will be initialized, and then the local 'client' can access the targeted server via its native protocols.

Lotus Notes Tunnel

The basic problem of connecting directly into a client/server-type application service is illustrated below using Lotus Notes, a popular application/messaging-based program (sometimes referred to as Domino) sold by IBM. Lotus Notes servers listen for client requests on TCP port 1352.

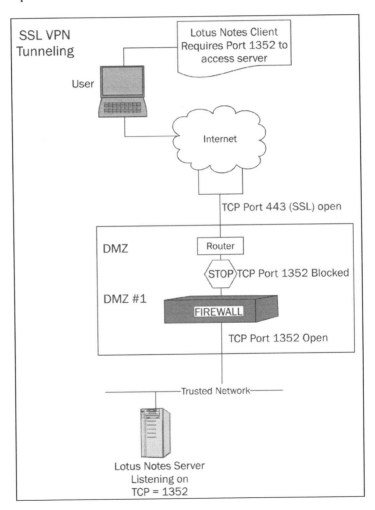

Tunneling Steps

The above example shows that the DMZ is blocking inbound Lotus Notes traffic. As stated, this company's DMZ rules state: "Direct application access via a TCP port is not allowed".

We can provide access and comply with the DMZ rule at the same time. An SSL VPN tunnel service can solve this access problem. Notes traffic can be embedded within SSL encrypted packets that travel on the standard HTTPS port as shown in the diagram below:

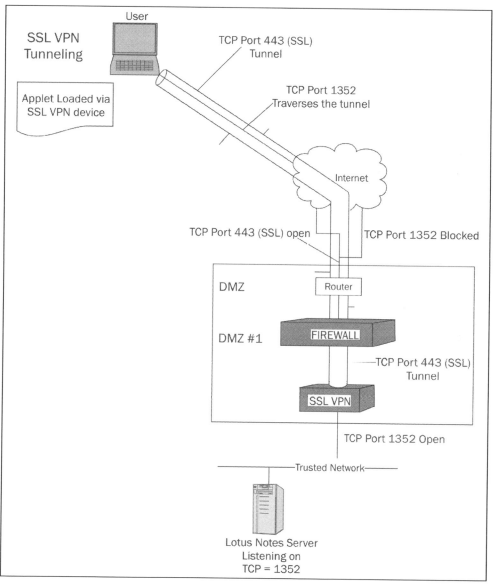

The steps to be followed by the end user are very simple:

1. The end user accesses the SSL VPN on a published URL (see RFC 1738) via a standard Internet browser, for example, `https://www.mycompanysite.com`.

2. The SSL VPN establishes an SSL-based session to the end user's browser.

3. The end user authenticates into the SSL VPN.

4. The end user selects the service required (say, Lotus Notes) from a menu list.

5. An applet is (downloaded if not already installed and) initialized.

6. The applet establishes an encrypted connection by connecting through port 443 (SSL) to the SSL VPN.

7. The applet on the end user's PC will now intercept Notes traffic destined for the user's target Notes server.

8. Lotus Notes traffic on port 1352 traverses the Internet TCP within the SSL encrypted packets sent to port 443 (SSL), destined for the SSL VPN.

9. The SSL VPN receives the data on port 443, extracts the Notes data, and then transfers the data to the native Lotus Notes port 1352.

Note that other methods of providing such access were described in Chapter 3 while discussing how SSL VPNs provide access to non-web applications.

Other Applications

SSL VPNs can provide a secure, on-demand access to most legacy-based applications. Very few applications will not translate onto a browser-based architecture via an SSL VPN. Very old database systems that have non-standard-based protocols and/or direct connection systems, and some LD proprietary protocols (e.g., X.PC), however, may pose some problems. In addition, applications that require large fat client downloads and updates and custom applications that run in kernel mode on a user's PC may not work from many machines. Of course, the physical abacus will likely not work over an SSL VPN either…

Summary

Most applications and services can be offered to end users across the Internet, via an SS VPN. Today's SSL VPN gateways consolidate key security features into a unified, hardened service. SSL VPNs can provide secure access to new applications as well as legacy applications.

8

The Future of SSL VPN Technology

Although SSL VPN technology has matured greatly since its inception, it has not yet reached its full potential. The process of development and meaningful enhancements is not yet complete. Technological improvements should prove to expand the capability and reliability of SSL VPN technology far beyond what it offers today.

Although many SSL VPN products started their lifetimes in similar forms, the various product vendors appear to have chosen several different paths for their product lines, which may ultimately yield very different products in the future. In addition, several technological advancements are presently occurring as this book goes to print. These improvements provide some insight as to what is in store for SSL VPN technology over the next 18 months.

In this chapter we will examine current trends in the SSL VPN marketplace and take a look at some potential future developments that may emerge as a result of those trends.

Standardized Feature Sets

One important point to realize is that although early versions of SSL VPN products offered greatly varied feature sets, today's leading offerings have relatively similar features. This is especially true when comparing features on paper (that is, as listed in marketing materials).

Part of the maturation process of each individual product is for its vendor to give it the ability to deliver the capabilities that the market demands, which often entails duplicating the functionality of competing offerings. As a result, the definition of what a product must offer to be considered an 'SSL VPN' is becoming increasingly clear and standardized with the passage of time.

Nonetheless, as was alluded to in earlier chapters, the underlying technology implementing the various features differs greatly from product to product. Such differences may affect the ease and speed at which a vendor can introduce desired features into its offering. As a result, as time passes, it is growing increasingly important for people looking to purchase an SSL VPN to review thoroughly what products under consideration really have to offer, what technologies they use to deliver access, and so on—not simply to make decisions based on marketing feature sheets.

Interfaces

Another important trend to be aware of while investing in an SSL VPN is that SSL VPNs are now beginning to offer interfaces for both, extending their capabilities and for integrating them with third-party products. These interfaces fall into several categories. Among these are:

- Third-party security interfaces
- Application interfaces
- Logging and reporting interfaces

Third-Party Security System Interfaces

One clear trend that has begun to develop is for SSL VPNs to offer interfaces to integrate with third-party security products. Security-related interfaces fall into several categories.

Authentication Systems

Authentication system interfaces allow organizations deploying SSL VPN technology to leverage existing authentication infrastructure and strong authentication systems such as RSA's SecurID. These systems were discussed in detail in Chapter 3. Such capabilities have been around since the early days of SSL VPN, and are not a new development. However, the one change that has come about as SSL VPNs continue to mature is the fact that it is now quite simple to integrate third-party authentication systems with an SSL VPN—this was not the case in the early days of SSL VPN technology. Additional authentication methods are likely to be seen in the future—perhaps even the use of biometric-based authentication for users wishing greater levels of access (see *Tiers of Access* in Chapter 3). Today, biometric readers are pretty sparse—most computers, for example, do not offer fingerprint readers. However, this may change in the future and, as it does, we can expect to see more biometric-based authentication used in conjunction with SSL VPNs. To address the reality that not all machines will gain biometric readers simultaneously, SSL VPNs may be configured to grant users authenticating with biometric devices a greater degree of access than their counterparts using username and password combinations. It should be noted that some forms of biometric-type authentication are already available from most computers—for example biometric systems that employ typing and keystroke dynamics. These forms of authentication examine the way users type and not just what they type. The intervals between key presses, the time for which keys are held down, the time delays between words, and many other factors can be examined so as to identify the patterns of individual users. There are already firms that are starting to offer such authentication capabilities and these systems will work from most computers.

Authorization Systems

Authorization system interfaces allow enterprises implementing an SSL VPN to utilize third-party authorization systems to manage user rights and permissions as well as other authorization information. Organizations with existing authorization systems do not need to replicate their data (which could lead to management issues and errors) if they use their existing infrastructure. Interfaces to third-party authorization systems have been around for some time, but the level of integration with SSL VPNs (i.e., how much information could be extracted from such systems and in how many ways could it be used) has certainly improved with time, and this is likely to continue as SSL VPN technology evolves.

Endpoint Security Systems

The first SSL VPN related endpoint security products entered the market in 2003, and, as such, SSL VPN interfaces to third-party endpoint security products are relatively new. Endpoint interfaces allow SSL VPN servers to communicate with third-party client-side software (either previously installed at the client or distributed via the SSL VPN) for enforcing client-side security. The third-party products may create secure environments on otherwise insecure machines, may wipe sensitive data from untrusted devices at the conclusion of SSL VPN user sessions, or may check for properly configured anti-virus software and personal firewalls. For more information on endpoint security, please see Chapter 3. As this book goes to print there are still significant developments taking place in the arena of SSL VPN endpoint security (partnerships, OEM agreements, etc.), and such activities are likely to continue for the near future.

Application Firewalling Interfaces

Some SSL VPNs come equipped with built-in application firewalls, while others do not. The year 2004 has brought business partnerships between SSL VPN vendors and application-firewall companies. It is likely that over the next year or so we will witness those SSL VPN vendors that do not yet have application firewalls add them to their products, provide interfaces to interface with third-party providers, or OEM third-party software and incorporate it into their SSL VPN products.

Application Interfaces

Application interfaces are relatively new; they allow SSL VPNs to communicate more easily and successfully with back-end applications, usually at the application level. The SSL VPN may offer a standard language for instructing it as to how to address various application idiosyncrasies. The SSL VPN might even offer a mechanism to create application-specific *modules* encapsulating different application information, or may provide other mechanisms for improving integration between the SSL VPN and back-end systems. Optimizing the integration of SSL VPN technology with applications is one area in which plenty of activity seems to be occurring. We can expect to see significant developments in this realm over the upcoming year.

Logging, Reporting, and Management Interfaces

There is little doubt that future improvements in SSL VPN technology will include enhanced reporting capabilities and the ability to manage SSL VPN servers using standard, centralized, management tools. The beginnings of these trends are already visible today.

Today's SSL VPNs typically offer some level of integration with standard reporting systems, but the degree to which they integrate certainly could use improvement. Some of today's SSL VPNs also offer **SNMP (Simple Network Management Protocol)** functionality, but likewise, their support for this standard management protocol is still sparse and incomplete. Standard log files are already generated by some SSL VPNs and can be processed with standard log processing tools, but not every item that customers may want to track is necessarily included in those log files and reports.

In the aforementioned areas related to reporting and management, we can expect to see dramatic improvements. Enhancements in these areas will be a natural byproduct of vendors' attempts to mature their offerings and help SSL VPN technology emerge from its place as a popular leading-edge technology into a mass-deployed standard component of corporate infrastructures around the globe.

> As this book goes to print, announcements of third-party products capable of producing reports from SSL VPN generated logs are beginning to appear. This is the beginning of a trend; you can expect to see more such reporting tools and SSL VPN integration capabilities in older reporting tools in the future.

SSL VPN Products for Small, Medium, and Large Organizations

One development already in progress is market segregation of SSL VPN appliances and software by the size of the organizations that each particular offering can support. Some SSL VPN appliances have performed better in large enterprise environments, others have excelled in smaller companies. As would be expected, the vendors that make such products have concentrated feature development and optimization around their customer base. As such, products that may have initially been similar in nature have evolved differently and grown apart over time.

In fact, some vendors that started with single 'one-size-fits-all' offerings have even released multiple appliances, with one model intended for sale to smaller firms and another version geared towards larger enterprises. Having a suite of offerings may be advantageous; firms with such a portfolio can conquer a larger segment of the remote-access market. At the same time, however, such an approach also poses drawbacks, as the lack of focus on a particular segment necessarily means that feature development cannot easily be optimized to meet the needs of a particular market. This can result in a vendor offering products incapable of providing all of the features that competing and specialized offerings may offer, and which particular organizations may require.

Application-Specific SSL VPNs

Some organizations, especially smaller firms, may have business requirements to implement remote access to only a single application, and may not require the robustness of a full SSL VPN platform. Under such circumstances, the cost of implementing a true SSL VPN may be prohibitive and an ROI-analysis may reveal that purchasing an SSL VPN may be unwise.

To address such situations, several SSL VPN vendors offer low-end SSL VPNs that support only one or two applications. Such products typically sell for far less than full-version SSL VPN appliances, and can often be upgraded to full SSL VPN functionality at a later date if the customer so desires. It is likely that additional SSL VPN vendors will begin to offer such solutions and that the vendors already marketing such products will continue to offer specialized appliances for additional applications.

Merging with IPSec VPN and Firewall Technology

There are two somewhat divergent approaches that SSL VPN vendors seem to be taking towards advancing their products, both of which are already in motion. Consideration should be given to these trends when selecting a vendor, as it is wise to ensure that your own strategic goal for SSL implementation (in addition to any tactical solution), is in sync with the aims of the vendor whose product you want to use. It is critical that technology be able to properly address changing and growing needs.

One potential future direction of SSL VPN may be the convergence of SSL VPN, Network Firewall, and IPSec VPN technology. IPSec has been merged with network firewall technology since its inception. SSL VPN began as an independent technology, but several observations in the current marketplace offer insight that a merger may ultimately occur:

1. In 2003-04, some SSL VPN vendors began to include network-type connectivity (as discussed in other sections of this book) within their product offerings. Such a capability makes the abilities of SSL VPN products much more closely parallel to those of IPSec VPN. It may also allow organizations to completely replace their User-to-Site IPSec VPN infrastructure with SSL VPN technology. In fact, some companies already have begun to do just that. How exactly the relationship of SSL VPN and IPSec VPN will play out will be determined over the course of time, but the trend towards SSL is clear. It is possible that over time SSL will displace IPSec as the dominant method for general User-to-Site remote access, while IPSec will be reserved for Site-to-Site connectivity and for special cases of User-to-Site access (such as for system administrators).

2. Netscreen, (`http://www.findarticles.com/p/articles/mi_m0PAT/is_2004_March/ai_114699561`) a major Firewall and IPSec VPN vendor, acquired one of the leading SSL VPN vendors (Neoteris). Although their SSL VPN and Firewall/IPSec VPN products today remain independent offerings, the potential for merging them into a unified product certainly exists. Netscreen has itself since been acquired by Juniper Networks.

3. Cisco, a major vendor of networking equipment, has released a free SSL add-on to its IPSec VPN concentrator. Although the SSL product may not technically be a full SSL VPN when compared to the features described throughout this book, it is certainly possible that future improved versions of the product will offer similar functionality to today's SSL VPNs. Of course, the product may remain a free add-on to the IPSec VPN concentrator or may evolve into an independent offering that Cisco might choose to sell.

4. Checkpoint, another Firewall and IPSec VPN vendor, announced in mid-2003 that it would release its own SSL VPN, and did so in mid-2004.

5. Microsoft has begun to incorporate some rudimentary HTML translation into its ISA firewall package. Although today the translation is far too limited to be classified as SSL VPN functionality, there is little doubt that if the SSL

VPN market remains hot, Microsoft might consider extending ISA's functionality to create an SSL VPN offering of its own.

6. Citrix, a maker of terminal-services type access products, acquired Net6—a newcomer to the SSL VPN space that offered a product Net6 described as a 'hybrid' of IPSec and SSL VPN technology.

All of these developments present a convincing story that Firewall/IPSec VPN vendors will grow increasingly involved with SSL VPN technology, and pose the potential for the convergence of the two technologies into unified offerings.

One interesting caveat: IPSec VPNs are usually run on network firewalls because the firewall regulates network-type connectivity to the internal network. When everything is working the way it is supposed to, users connect to the Internet and their corporate network seamlessly. A well-configured IPSec VPN concentrator is essentially invisible to users. As such it makes sense to run IPSec VPN technology on a network firewall. SSL VPN is completely different, however. Users are supposed to interact with an SSL VPN server—it provides them with various menus, bookmarks, and so on. Installing SSL capabilities onto a network firewall means that users will necessarily need to interact with the firewall server, making it clearly visible to users, something that many security-conscious organizations may frown upon.

It would also seem that companies proceeding along the path toward convergence of networking and application-level access are concentrating on providing access for employees (and potentially other trusted parties) to more systems than currently possible. In other words, they are concentrating on the same group of people that IPSec and SSL VPNs currently focus on. However, are expanding their technology to offer access to just as many resources and from more locations than IPSec *without* the maintenance demands and general complexity of IPSec. This will differ greatly from another observable trend as discussed in the next section.

The convergence of SSL application-level technology with network-level communications will allow employees to remotely access from web browsers many more resources than previously possible (as pictured below). The incorporation of firewall technologies into SSL VPN systems (or of SSL VPN systems into firewalls) may also help alleviate some of the security concerns of establishing network connectivity over SSL as described in chapters 3 and 4.

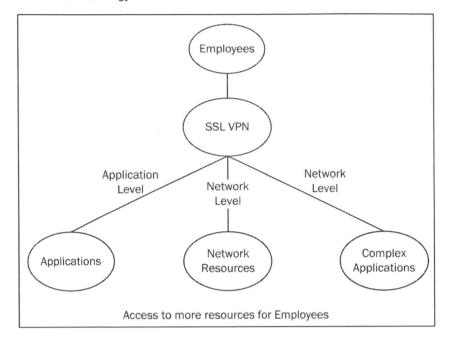

Access to more resources for Employees

SSL Access Platforms

Remote Access for employees is an important use of the Web, but there are numerous other business purposes for which SSL-type connectivity can be utilized. Besides the obvious purpose of on-line commerce, SSL access can also be used for interaction with partners and customers. For example, equipment manufacturers may make available design information to companies 'OEMing' their technology, law firms may share documents with clients, medical insurance companies may offer remote access to medical-claim information (to patients, their lawyers, and other insurance companies), insurance companies may allow 401(k)-plan and IRA participants the ability to remotely manage retirement accounts held at their firms. All of these activities can be automated, and made more convenient for users, by leveraging the World Wide Web. Of course, in each case security and privacy are of paramount concern.

> **OEMing** refers to a business model in which Company A re-labels a product that it sells, but which was made by Company B, so that is appears to the marketplace that Company A made the product.

Although the business goals of the aforementioned systems differ greatly from the classic understanding of the function of an SSL VPN, adding several enhancements to SSL VPN technology can make an SSL VPN server a powerful gateway to provide secure remote access into such systems. Some SSL VPN products seem to be heading in the direction of becoming such SSL Access Platforms.

To be able to deliver access for many different groups of users to internal resources an SSL VPN must obviously be able to provide access to a large number of applications at the application level and support multiple concurrent SSL access portals. Contrast this with the scenario described earlier of the trend toward providing access to many more resources but only for employees; a very different path of SSL VPN maturation is clearly being followed. The goal of the vendors attempting to create SSL Access Platforms is primarily to expand the group of users who will use the system. Increasing the types of access a particular group of users can achieve, beyond the already large number of accessible resources, is a secondary concern. Of course, in reality most vendors' decisions as to the development path of their products will not be fully in either direction. Even the vendors focusing on convergence are trying to expand their application-level support of applications, and even firms that are growing their products into SSL Access Platforms are ensuring that they can provide low-level or network-level access to internal resources.

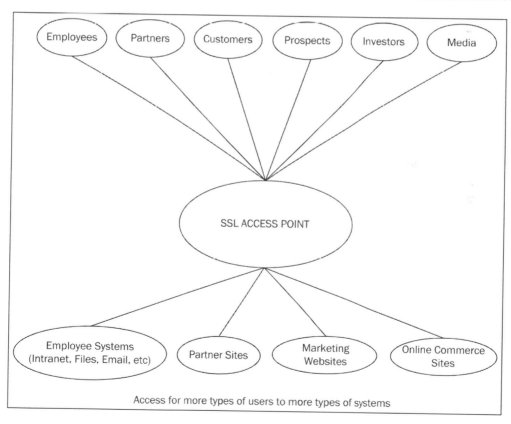

As shown above, SSL Access Platforms—an expanded version of SSL VPNs—may become standard SSL gateways for all web-based business purposes much as network firewalls have become for guarding all network entry points into an organization.

Support for More Diverse Computers

The current and future support of SSL VPNs of remote access from various platforms and computing devices is discussed in the following sections.

Macintosh

Quite clearly, those SSL VPNs that do not yet support access from Macintosh computers are likely to add such support. (Many SSL VPNs today offer limited access capabilities from Macintosh machines. The level of access is likely to increase as newer SSL VPN versions are released.)

Linux and Other Variants of UNIX

As was the case with Macintosh computers, SSL VPN support for remote access from machines running Linux and other flavors of UNIX is currently limited. It is reasonable to expect that such support will be expanded in the future.

Handheld Devices

The ability to access important systems and information from anywhere has grown dramatically with the development and delivery of Internet-enabled handled devices.

Internet-enabled **Personal Data Assistants (PDAs)** and other handheld devices continue to proliferate at a rapid pace. People love the convenience of being able to access online resources from devices that they can carry with them everywhere they go. The sophistication of today's handheld computers and the processing power now available in small, portable, form factors enables SSL VPN technology to provide access from devices that fit in users' pockets. In fact, many SSL VPN products now offer technology to accommodate access from systems running operating environments such as WindowsCE/Pocket PC, PalmOS, and Symbian.

One important technical feature offered by SSL VPN technology is the ability to adjust the SSL VPN GUI based on the type of device used for access. It is obvious that on a small device a web browser cannot possibly display a full-sized browser screen in a readable format; a miniature interface is necessary. Also, in the case of many web-enabled cellular phones, wireless bandwidth constraints (when using cellular networks) can render intolerable the time it takes to load graphically rich pages or other multimedia that may be used over the wired Internet; fewer images and sounds are common in handheld-optimized web pages.

One point to note—today's SSL VPNs do not typically offer the same degree of access from handheld devices as they do from regular computers. Although most SSL VPNs do support access to web-based applications from small devices, due to the limitations of the devices, they often do not support network-level connectivity or other forms of access to non-web applications. Mounting of remote drives is also not usually available (although a file-access GUI may be). Most of these shortcomings stem from the inability of many handheld devices to run the ActiveX or Java controls necessary to implement full remote access. Nonetheless, as many key applications now offer web interfaces, the ability to access web-based applications from handheld devices can prove quite valuable to an organization. In addition, as vendors produce new generations of handheld devices, and as new versions of SSL VPN appliances/software are released to the marketplace, these shortcomings may disappear.

It is clear that in the future we will see expanded capabilities in the area of access from handheld devices to important resources via SSL VPN technology.

Improved Performance and Reliability

As has been the case with many other technologies, SSL VPN technology continues to grow faster and more reliable as it matures. This is due to three primary factors:

- SSL VPN vendors are leveraging faster hardware as it becomes available (and less expensive).

- SSL VPN vendors are increasingly offering performance and reliability improving technology within their offerings. SSL accelerators, load balancers, and the like are becoming standard components of SSL VPN offerings. Caching performed by SSL VPN servers to improve performance is also likely to become more common with time.

- As SSL VPN software is utilized by a growing number of organizations, it is subjected to more-and-more real-world use. Bugs within product design and code are discovered and corrected. In addition, any incompatibilities with specific applications are also able to be detected and repaired. This trend toward improved reliability and performance will certainly continue.

It is also possible that some companies that are vendors of SSL Acceleration products will incorporate SSL VPN capabilities into their offerings further blending the two technologies.

Voice-Over-IP

There has been some talk of late of delivering **Voice-Over-IP (VoIP)** access to remote sites using an SSL VPN. Although such a capability sounds quite interesting, to date, it has not been a significant factor in the SSL VPN marketplace. As VoIP becomes more widely deployed, this may change.

Two "Business Developments"

Although not technically part of the "future of SSL VPN technology", two important observations that should be made when discussing the future of SSL VPN are:

1. Many organizations that have purchased SSL VPNs initially deployed SSL VPN access to only small portions of their respective companies. It is likely that over the next few years these firms will roll out SSL VPN access to much greater portions of their entire organizations.

2. It is likely that there will be further consolidation of the SSL VPN marketplace with mergers and acquisitions of SSL VPN vendors quite probable.

Summary

In this chapter we examined several emerging trends in the SSL VPN market and their influence on the future developments. We discussed:

- New interfacing capabilities with third-party security, application, and management systems
- The emergence of different SSL VPN products for different sized organizations
- Application-specific SSL VPNs
- The two directions SSL VPN products seem to be heading in—convergence with networking technologies such as network firewalls and becoming application-level access platforms
- SSL VPN access from handheld devices
- Overall maturation of SSL VPN technology and the improved performance that goes along with it

We wish you the best of luck with your SSL VPN implementation!

A Review of TCP, IP, and Ports

DARPA and OSI

Overall, there is no formal correlation between the TCP protocol model and the OSI model. But, they are roughly equivalent in the services that are provided. The following diagram shows a comparison between the models:

Protocol Implementation				
DARPA Layer				**OSI**
Process/ Application	FTP		TFTP	**Application**
	SMTP		NFS	**Presentation**
		TELNET	SNMP	**Session**
	RFC: 959, 821, 854		RFC: 783, 1094	
Transport	Transmission Protocol (TCP) RFC793		User Datagram Protocol (UDP) RFC768	**Transport**
Internet	(ARP) Address Resolution RFC826, 903	(IP) Internet Protocol RFC791	Internet Control Message Protocol RFC792	**Network**
Network Interface	Network Interface Cards: Ethernet, Token Ring RFC894 RFC1024			**Data Link**
	Transmission Twisted Pair, Coax, Fiber, Wireless, etc.			**Physical**

Network Interface

The first layer of the DARPA model is the Network Interface Layer; it links the local host to the local network hardware. This loosely maps to the Physical and Data Link layers of the OSI reference model. The Network Interface Layer makes the physical connection to the network, be it wireless, Ethernet cables, or Token Ring cables (an IBM legacy protocol). In each case a frame is generated with data from the upper layers. The Internet Layer transfers the packets between systems (or hosts). A host, in this definition, can be a client, server, or a peer in a peer-to-peer transfer. Each packet will contain address information relating to the source and destination of the packet. The Transport Layer is responsible for providing communication between applications residing on different hosts. This can also be called the host-to-host layer. Depending on the application, the Transport Layer will provide two types of service—a reliable service (TCP) or an unreliable service (UDP). In a reliable service the receiving station acknowledges the receipt of a datagram. The unreliable service does not provide a mechanism to acknowledge packets. The top layer of the DARPA model is the Application Layer. This is where actual applications like Trivial File Transfer Protocol and Telnet reside.

TFTP and Telnet

Trivial File Transfer Protocol (TFTP) is a simple form of the FTP. TFTP uses the UDP and provides no security features. It is often used by servers to boot diskless workstations, X-terminals, and routers. **Telnet** is a terminal emulation program for TCP/IP networks such as the Internet. The Telnet program runs on your computer and connects your PC to a server on the network. You can then enter commands through the Telnet program and they will be executed as if you were entering them directly on the server console. This enables you to control the server and communicate with other servers on the network. To start a Telnet session, you must log in to a server by entering a valid username and password. Telnet is a common way to control web servers remotely.

Packets

So we have seen a network packet and where it lives in the TCP/IP model. Next let's look at the IP packet. The IP packet is how the TCP packet finds which computer it is destined for. The Internet Protocol is defined in RFC 791 (http://info.internet.isi.edu:80/ in-notes/rfc/files/rfc791.txt). IP provides the most basic level of service in the Internet. IP is the basis upon which the other protocols stand. IP provides the protocol above it with a basic service model. IP is similar to a postal service (like the ones in which you get your bills). Using an address scheme, a packet is routed from a source to a destination, much like a letter having a street address. Overall IP does not promise a perfect network connectivity service, hence it is known as a **Best Effort Service**. If you send a postal message from your house, you rely on this *best effort* believing that your message will arrive at its destination. Without special handling you will not know if the letter (like your utility bill) has been delivered to its intended destination.

Packet Routing

Once the packet has been created, it is routed from a source system to a target system:

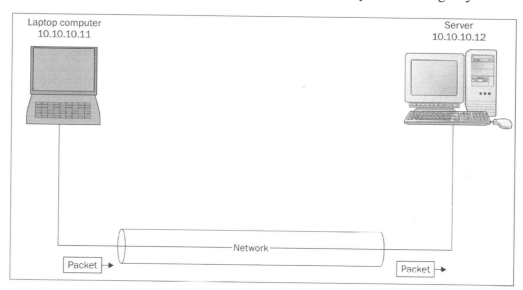

In this example, the Laptop computer is sending an IP packet to the Server. The Source IP Address is 10.10.10.11 and the Target address is 10.10.10.12. Using this nomenclature the server now knows how to respond back to the Laptop computer. This address scheme is how computers talk to each other on the Internet or any IP network. So back to our postal analogy: the IP address is much like the address on the letter, or the address of your house. So the letter (packet) is dropped into the postal box and it is sent via a network of postal employees, with one finally dropping the letter at your house or mailbox. In this example we have delivered a message to your house. But how do we know the person that should be receiving the message? This same question and its subsequent solution also present themselves in networking. TCP rides in the network packet after the IP packet. The TCP packet contains information about the application. Although IP routes packets through the Internet using the destination address, more information is needed to identify which application on the destination host should receive the data once it arrives. This is accomplished via ports.

TCP Ports

Both sending and receiving applications are assigned **port numbers** to send and receive data. Coupled with the source and destination IP address, the source and destination port number, a small integer number, identifies which application is associated with any given data transfer. As mentioned before, the IP address is like the addressing scheme of a postal service. Once the Postal Service delivers the letter to your house, further addressing on the letter (the recipient's name which appears above the destination address) determines who actually gets the letter. This is where TCP helps out. The TCP port addresses (source and target) provide a mechanism to direct data to a specific application. Once the IP packet arrives at the host then the port determines which application receives the data. The addressing scheme in IP uses 2 bytes of data to determine how to deliver the message. With 2 bytes (16 bits) of data you can have up to 65,000 different ports per IP address—that is, 65,000 different recipients per IP Address.

Port numbers are divided into three ranges:

- **Well Known Ports**: 0 through 1023
- **Registered Ports**: 1024 through 49151
- **Dynamic and/or Private Ports**: 49152 through 65535

To ensure consistency across networks, the **Internet Assigned Numbers Authority** (**IANA**: http://www.iana.org/) assigns specific port numbers to popular applications. The port numbers are known as **well-known port numbers** and are de facto standards. For that reason, you can expect SMTP mail service to always be available on port 25, NNTP news service to be on port 119, HTTP to be served on port 80, HTTPS encrypted web traffic to be sent on port 443, Telnet to be available via port 23, and so on. For more information on well known port assignments please consult http://www.iana.org/assignments/port-numbers.

The use of ports is actually a very simple process. In the TCP world there is a **listener device** (that listens for communications sent to a specific port number) and the **instantiation device** (that establishes communication to a specific address and port number). One example would be a client and a server. The server would be the listener, example: port 80 for an HTTP web server. The client, in this example, would use a random port to communicate out to the server's port 80. The random port used by the client is known as an **ephemeral port number**. Ephemeral ports are temporary ports assigned by a machine's TCP/IP stack, and are assigned from a pre-determined range of ports. When the TCP connection terminates, the use of the client (ephemeral) port is terminated and then is available for reuse.

B

SSL VPN Gateways

SSL VPN Offerings

The following is a list of vendors offering SSL VPN gateways and some information about their offerings. Some of the companies mentioned below are relatively new to the SSL VPN space; others have been around for a while. Some of the products are quite robust; others offer only basic feature-sets. To find out more, we recommend visiting the respective vendor web sites and/or contacting the vendors.

All the information in this appendix was taken from various publicly available sources and is correct to the best of our knowledge at the time of writing the book (December 2004). If you find any errors or would like to see any other dates to this section, please email us at the Feedback address given in the Introduction.

AEP Systems

www.aepsystems.com

Company Information

AEP Systems Inc.

100 Hamilton Ave

Palo Alto, CA 94301

Toll Free: 1.800.383.7716

Tel: (+1) 650.326.6748

Fax: (+1) 650.326.6806

Product Information

Appliances:

- A-Gate AG-50 (small companies)
- A-Gate AG-60 (small to mid-size companies)
- A-Gate AG-600 (small to mid-size companies)
- A-Gate AG-1200 (mid-size to large companies)

On December 22, 2004, AEP Systems announced a merger with Netilla Networks (mentioned later in this chapter). As of the printing of this book, however, both SSL VPN product lines are still being marketed.

Array Networks

www.arraynetworks.net

Company Information

254 East Hacienda Ave.

Campbell, CA 95008

Phone: 408-378-6800

Fax: 408-874-2753

Toll Free: 866-692-7729

Product Information

Appliances:

- Array SP-C (all sized companies)
- Array SPX2000 (small to mid-size companies)
- Array SPX300 (mid-size to large companies)
- Array SP (large companies)

Aventail

www.aventail.com

Company Information

808 Howell St., 2nd Fl.

Seattle, WA 98101

Phone: 206-215-1111

Fax: 206-215-1120

Toll Free: 877-283-6824

Product Information

Appliances:

- EX-750 (small companies)
- EX-1500 (mid-size to large companies)

Managed Service:

- SA-1000 (small-scale)
- SA-9000 (large-scale)

Check Point Software Technologies

www.checkpoint.com

Company Information

800 Bridge Pkwy

Redwood City, CA 94065

Phone: 650-628-2000

Fax: 650-654-4233

Product Information

Appliances:

- Connectra 1000 (small companies)
- Connectra 2000 (mid-size to large companies)
- Connectra 6000 (large companies)

Cisco Systems

www.cisco.com

Company Information

170 W. Tasman Dr.

San Jose, CA 95134

Phone: 408-526-4000

Fax: 408-526-4100

Toll Free: 800-326-1941

Product Information

Cisco WebVPN for Cisco VPN 3000 Series Concentrator (add-on to IPSEC VPN Concentrator)

Citrix Systems
www.citrix.com

Company Information
Citrix Systems, Inc.

851 West Cypress Creek Road

Fort Lauderdale, Florida 33309

Phone: 954-267-3000

Fax: 954-267-9319

Toll Free: 800-424-8749

Product Information
Appliances:

- Citrix (Net6) Hybrid-VPN Gateway

Citrix Systems acquired Net6 (announced November 23, 2004)

EnKoo

www.enkoo.com

Company Information

4046 Clipper Court

Fremont, CA 94538

Phone: (510) 770-8509

Fax: (510) 770-0475

Product Information

Appliance

- EnKoo-1000 (small companies)
- EnKoo-2000 (small companies)
- EnKoo-3000 (small to mid-size companies)

F5 Networks

www.f5.com

Company Information

401 Elliott Ave. West

Seattle, WA 98119

Phone: 206-272-5555

Fax: 206-272-5556

Toll Free: 888-882-4447

Product Information

FirePass Controller

F5 acquired uRoam (July 23, 2003)

Juniper Networks

www.juniper.net

Company Information

1194 North Mathilda Ave.

Sunnyvale, CA 94089

Phone: 408-745-2000

Fax: 408-745-2100

Toll Free: 888-586-4737

Original company name: Danastreet

Renamed: Neoteris (September 2001)

Acquired by: Netscreen Technologies (Announced: October 6, 2003; Completed: November 17, 2003)

Acquired by: Juniper Networks (Announced: February 9, 2004; Completed: April 16, 2004)

Product Information

Appliances:

- Netscreen Remote Access 500 (small companies)
- Netscreen Secure Access 1000 (small to mid-size companies)
- Netscreen Secure Access 3000 (mid-size to large companies)
- Netscreen Secure Access 5000 (large companies)

NetScaler

www.netscaler.com

Company Information

2880 San Tomas Expressway, Suite 200

Santa Clara, CA 95051

Phone: 408-987-8700

Fax: 408-987-8701

Product Information

Appliance:

- NetScaler 9000 Series

NetSilica

www.netsilica.com

Company Information

377 Hoes Lane

Ste 260

Piscataway, NJ 08854-4138

Phone: 732-465-1400

Product Information

Appliances:

- NetSilica EPN Appliance

Software:

- NetSilica EPN Software

Netilla Networks

www.netilla.com

Company Information

347 Elizabeth Ave Ste 100

Somerset, NJ 08873-1123

Phone: 732-652-5200

Product Information

Appliance:

- Netilla Secure Gateway Appliance SGA (General SSL VPN)
- Netilla Secure Gateway Appliance SGA-C (SSL VPN for Citrix)

On December 22, 2004, AEP Systems announced a merger with Netilla Networks (mentioned later in this chapter). As of the printing of this book, however, both SSL VPN product lines are still being marketed.

Nokia

www.nokia.com

Company Information

Keilalahdentie 4

FIN-00045 Espoo, Finland

Phone: +358-7180-08000

Fax: +358-7180-38226

Product Information

Appliance:

- Nokia Secure Access System

Nortel Networks

www.nortel.com

Company Information

8200 Dixie Rd., Ste. 100

Brampton, Ontario L6T 5P6, Canada

Phone: 905-863-0000

Fax: 905-863-8408

Toll Free: 800-466-7835

Product Information

Appliance:

- VPN Gateway 3050

Permeo Technologies

www.permeo.com

Company Information

6535 N. State Highway 161, Bldg. A, 5th Fl.

Irving, TX 75039

Phone: 214-262-4600

Fax: 214-262-4651

Toll Free: 866-473-7636

> Permeo was spun off from NEC USA.

Product Information

Appliance:

- Permeo Application Security Gateway

PortWise

www.portwise.com

Company Information

PortWise AB

Mail P.O. Box 4146

102 63 Stockholm, Sweden

Phone: +46 (0)8 562 914 00

Fax: +46 (0)8 642 53 99

Product Information

Software:

- PortWise mVPN

SafeNet

www.safenet-inc.com

Company Information

4690 Millennium Drive

Belcamp, MD 21017

Telephone: 410-931-7500

Fax: 410-931-7524

Product Information

Appliance:

- SafeEnterprise SSL iGate

Symantec
www.symantec.com

Company Information
20330 Stevens Creek Blvd.

Cupertino, CA 95014-2132

Phone: 408-517-8000

Fax: 408-253-3968

Symantec acquired Safeweb (October 20, 2003)

Product Information
Appliance:

- Symantec Clientless VPN Gateway 4400 Series

Whale Communications

www.whalecommunications.com

Company Information

400 Kelby Street, 15th Floor

Fort Lee, NJ 07024

Phone: 201-947-9177

Fax: 201-947-9188

Toll Free: 877-659-4253

Product Information

Appliances:

- e-Gap Webmail Appliance (Email specific SSL VPN)
- e-Gap Remote Access Appliance (Full SSL VPN—mid-size to large companies)

Index

Made in the USA
Lexington, KY
26 January 2012